BBC **MATCH OF THE DAY**

D0490221

MATCH OF THE DAY
Annual 2015

This book belongs to: BEN CHURCH

Age: 8/9

My favourite team is: LIVERPOOL

My favourite player is: MESSI

My highlight of 2014 was: WORLD CUP

WELCOME!

We can safely say that 2014 was an amazing year for football, full of drama, excitement and amazing action. You can relive it all with this MOTD Annual 2015 – and it looks like 2015 could be ever better. Happy reading!

2014: A QUICK REMINDER!

● Man. City won their second title in three years ● Arsenal won the FA Cup, their first trophy for nine years
● Real Madrid were Champions League winners ● Germany beat Argentina in the World Cup Final
● England crashed out in the group stage ● Ryan Giggs retired after 23 years at Man. United

LUIS SUAREZ
AND HIS UTTERLY RIDICULOUS 2014!

20 APRIL
His 30th goal of the season puts Liverpool five points clear!

27 APRIL
He's named PFA Player Of The Year!

5 MAY
Sobs as Liverpool throw away a three-goal lead against Crystal Palace!

11 MAY
Man. City are crowned champions!

WHAT'S INSIDE

p6 The Colombian who's taking over the world!

p16 Why is Arsene Wenger hunting an owl?

p44 The rapid rise of rapid Raheem!

p51 The only way to deal with cats in 2015?

p61 What do Ron and a pyramid have in common?

WHAT'S ^not INSIDE

How to be a world-class manager! BY **DAVID MOYES**

How to win the Prem! BY **STEVEN GERRARD**

How to be a deadly striker! BY **FERNANDO TORRES**

How to keep your best players! BY **RONALD KOEMAN**

How to not get injured! BY **ANDY CARROLL**

PLUS loads, loads more!

22 MAY He's a World Cup doubt after emergency knee surgery!

19 JUNE But he returns to help knock England out of the World Cup!

24 JUNE Then he decides to bite an Italian!

26 JUNE And gets banned by FIFA for four months!

16 JULY But that doesn't stop Barcelona signing him for £75 million!

JAMES

the birth of a global phenomenon!

THIS IS THE STORY OF HOW **JAMES RODRIGUEZ** WENT FROM TALENTED YOUNGSTER TO A £63 MILLION MEGASTAR!

TURN OVER TO FIND OUT HOW HE DID IT! →

FOLLOWING IN THE FOOTSTEPS OF GIANTS!

Real Madrid love to break the bank to lure the world's best players to the Bernabeu — here are the most expensive superstars in their 112-year history!

1 GARETH BALE
£86 million
FROM: TOTTENHAM
WHEN: SEPTEMBER 2013
The Prem Player Of the Year makes a dramatic deadline day switch to Spain for a world-record transfer fee!

2 CRISTIANO RONALDO
£80 million
FROM: MAN. UNITED
WHEN: JULY 2009
Man. United finally agree to sell Ron – he signs a six-year deal and at the time it's the biggest-ever transfer!

3 JAMES RODRIGUEZ
£63 million
FROM: MONACO
WHEN: JULY 2014
After bossing the World Cup in Brazil, James tells his club Monaco he wants to join Real – and he gets his wish!

4 KAKA
£56 million
FROM: AC MILAN
WHEN: JUNE 2009
The Brazil star agrees to sign for Real in a then world-record deal – after turning down Man. City six months earlier!

JAMES

MAKING THE HEADLINES!

Rodriguez burst onto the scene in Brazil at the World Cup – but why was everyone talking about him?

■ He was the tournament's top scorer with **SIX** goals in five games!

■ He was named man of the match in **THREE** of the four games he played!

■ He picked up **TWO** assists – only four players made more in the tournament!

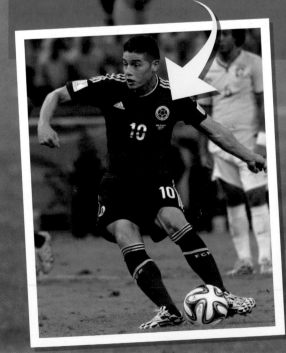

JAMES & HIS GIANT MOVE!

Just 12 months after joining Monaco for £37m, he made his dream move to Real following an amazing World Cup. They splashed out £63m to sign him – making him the fourth-most expensive player of all time. 45,000 fans turned up to watch him sign!

THE ULTIMATE No.10!

James is a throwback to the traditional No.10 playmaker. He's not blessed with electric pace, but he doesn't need it – his touch, technique and control mean he's always got time on the ball. The new Real star can pick a pass as well as anyone and he chips in with spectacular goals, too!

THE ROAD TO REAL!

2007-2008 ENVIGADO	2008-2010 BANFIELD	2010-2013 PORTO	2013-2014 MONACO
30 GAMES	42 GAMES	63 GAMES	34 GAMES
9 GOALS	5 GOALS	25 GOALS	9 GOALS
	£250,000	£4 MILLION	£35 MILLION

OOH, THEY LOVE A SELFIE!

SNAP!

It's time for the top five footy selfies of 2014!

1 PABLO IN A WIG WITH A BLOODY LIP!

Wow, look at the state of him! He hasn't just got home from a boozy night out in Manchester – it's taken in the Argentina dressing room after their bruising World Cup semi-final against Holland!

2 NEYMAR AND THE BRAZILIANS!

Neymar is a prolific selfie snapper – but this was our fave of his 2014 pics. Do you ever wonder what dinner time is like if you're a footballer? Well, wonder no more!

3 MLS STAR — DURING A GAME!

That's right, Kansas City striker Dom Dwyer scored, legged it over to the fans and took this selfie to celebrate. The ref wasn't very happy, though – he booked Dwyer for it!

4 RONALDO AND HIS PORTUGEEZERS!

This is too good. You've got C-Ron's cheesy grin, Nani's excited eyeballs and, of course, slap-bang in the centre, you've got Raul Meireles – and the best beard in football!

5 THE DROG ON THE BENCH!

There's not enough larking around on the subs' bench for our liking – so we're big fans of Didier Drogba's cheeky snap of himself and his fellow bench-warmers!

FUNNIES

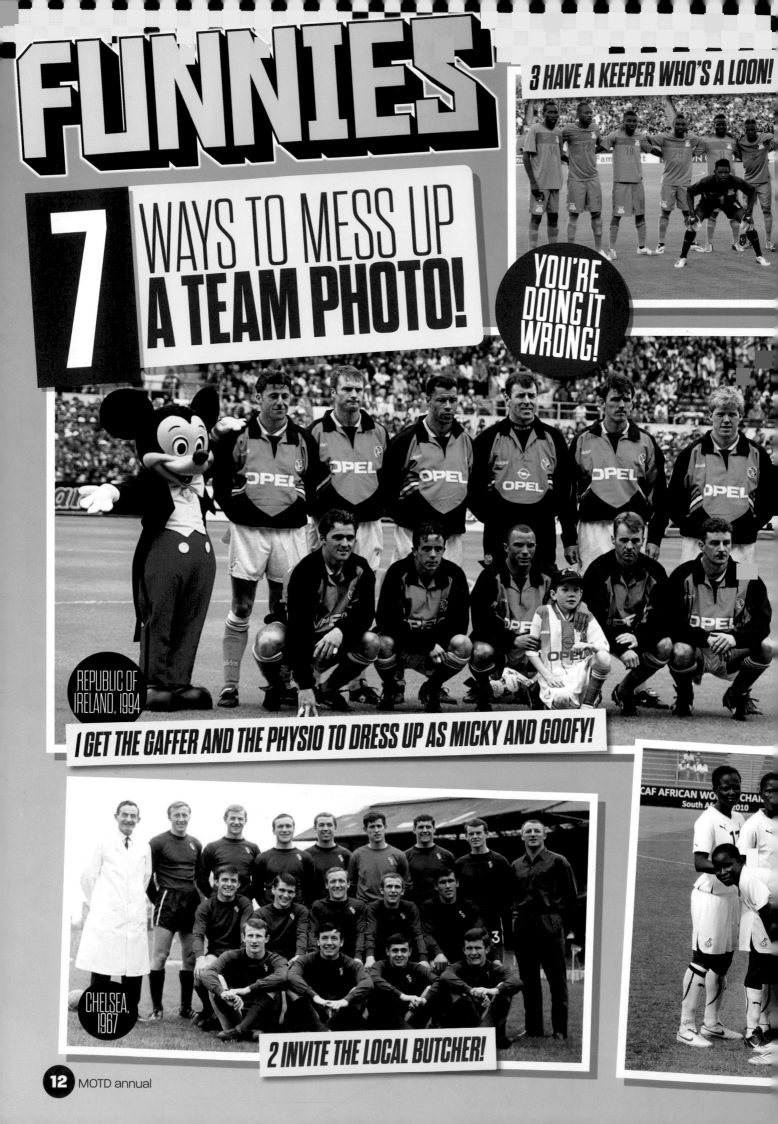

7 WAYS TO MESS UP A TEAM PHOTO!

YOU'RE DOING IT WRONG!

REPUBLIC OF IRELAND, 1994

1 GET THE GAFFER AND THE PHYSIO TO DRESS UP AS MICKY AND GOOFY!

CHELSEA, 1967

2 INVITE THE LOCAL BUTCHER!

CAF AFRICAN WO... CHA... South Af... 2010

ZAMBIA, 2014

MUNICH 1860, 2000

4 FACE THE WRONG WAY!

FC TWENTE, 1974

5 DON'T BUY ENOUGH KITS!

COLOMBIA, 2013

6 FORGET TO BOOK A BABYSITTER!

GHANA WOMEN, 2010

7 START DOING THE CONGA!

A DOG'S LIFE!

SAY WOOF TO CARLOS TEVEZ DOG!

SAY WOOF TO NEYMAR DOG!

IMAGINE IF LUIS SUAREZ WAS A BINMAN NOT A £70m MAN!

REFS SPRAY THE FUNNIEST THINGS!

THE MOTD Crossword!

Forget those boring crosswords that old people do, here's a special footy one for you!

4 Across: M A N C I T Y

12: T W E L V E

4 ACROSS

6 DOWN

GET THE ANSWERS ON p92!

ACROSS

4 The current holders of the League Cup! (3, 4)

7 Man. United finished in this position last season! (7)

8 Mark Noble's club! (4, 3)

10 Everton's captain is Phil _____! (8)

12 Mesut Ozil's shirt number at Arsenal! (6)

DOWN

1 Stoke are also known as The _____! (7)

2 Hull play their home games at the ___ Stadium! (1, 1)

3 Chelsea's Diego Costa plays for this country! (5)

5 The Tottenham manager's surname! (10)

6 Liverpool signed Lazar Markovic from this club! (7)

9 Southampton's nickname! (6)

11 Swansea play at the _____ Stadium! (7)

▶▶▶ TURN TO PAGE 30 FOR MORE QUIZ ACTION!

FOOTY'S TV TAKE

SATURDAY

Come Dine With Mee
3pm BBC One
Burnley's Ben Mee rustles up a slowly braised lamb shank in this week's episode. Guests include England physio Gary Lewin, astrologer Russell Grant and Mexico boss Miguel Herrera.

That's the Way To Do It: Puncheon Judy
4pm CBBC
Crystal Palace's flying winger Jason Puncheon embarks on a whistle-stop tour of English seaside resorts to discover his family's role in the creation of the chaotic Punch & Judy puppet show.

Lallanas In Pyjamas
8pm BBC One
Adam Lallana and his mum continue their attempt to run up and down every escalator in Liverpool. Listen out for Lallana's now-famous 'Oi, oi, saveloy!' catchphrase.

Catt Amongst The Pigeons
6pm BBC One
Sunderland midfielder Lee Cattermole enters the fifth week of his survival marathon, locked up in a garden shed with just his bread-hat and 37 feral pigeons for company.

SUNDAY

Join The Dots
7am BBC One
EastEnders' Dot Branning and snooker player Graham Dott host their award-winning breakfast show analysing the tactics and talking points from Saturday's Premier League action.

Gonzalo's Goat
10am BBC Two
Weeks of training will be put to the test as Gonzalo Higuain attempts to complete the London Marathon – on the back of his pet goat Gerald. Their near-death experience on the M25 will seem a million miles away if he does.

Carl, Jarl And Big Bad Van Gaal
8.30pm BBC One
Hold on to your hats! West Ham's Carl Jenkinson, young Swedish defender Gustav Jarl and United boss Louis Van Gaal continue their tour of Thailand. This week, they run amok in the country's capital, Bangkok.

MONDAY

New: Cheick Mate
7pm BBC Two
Newcastle's Cheick Tiote starts his quest to become a chess grand master by competing in the Northumberland heats – but not all is as it seems.

New: Oops, That'll Be The Sausages
7.30pm BBC Three
The popular hit sit-com returns with Robert Snodgrass and Wilfried Bony as the Blackpool-based crime-fighting duo Bangers & Mash.

Welbeck's Do Not Try This At Home
8pm BBC Three
The England striker tries to drink a pint of milk through a trumpet while playing the banjo in the latest of his wild and wacky world-record attempts.

FILM HIGHLIGHTS

Harry Redknapp & The Goblet Of Fire
★★★★★
5pm BBC One
QPR boss Harry Redknapp has to to use his wizardry skills when he competes against rival schools of magic in a dangerous and mysterious tournament.

Roy Story
★★★
7pm BBC One
The madcap adventures of England manager Roy Hodgson, Buzz Lightyear, Mr Potato Head, Rex and a host of discarded toys.

Slumdog Mignolet
★★★★★
8pm BBC One
The Liverpool keeper becomes a surprise contestant on Who Wants To Be A Millionaire?

OVER

We imagine the ultimate week of telly

TUESDAY

Bargain Hunt: Aston Villa Special

11.30am BBC One

Villa boss Paul Lambert visits a car boot sale in York in search of free transfers and injury-prone players.

Time Team: The Search For Howard Webb's Hair

7pm BBC One

Tony Robinson leads a team of historians and archaeologists across Yorkshire as they hunt for the ref's missing barnet.

Jamie's 30-Minute Meals USA

8pm BBC Three

Jamie Carragher eats his way across the USA, tackling a string of gut-busting challenges. This week, can he scoff Greasy Betty's giant burger pizza in half an hour?

Teenage Mutant Ninja Skrtels ★★

7pm BBC One

Four mutant Martin Skrtels fight to save the city from petty criminals and evil overlords.

WEDNESDAY

Horrid Henry

8am CBBC

Thierry Henry stars in a real-life version of the popular illustrated children's book. In this episode he gets involved in a fight with the tooth fairy.

BFC Finals

7pm BBC Four

Coverage of the opening match of the badger five-a-side football championships, live from Butlins in Minehead. Subsequent programmes may run late.

New: Owl Chase

9pm BBC One

Join Arsene Wenger on Clapham Common as he tries to catch an owl armed only with a frying pan and a pogo stick. New series, hosted by Chris Packham.

James And The Giant Peach ★★★

5pm BBC Two

The Colombian befriends a group of bugs living in a giant peach – and joins them on a trip to New York.

THURSDAY

Ron Vlaar And His Imaginary Car

5pm BBC Two

Slapstick comedy starring the big Dutch centre-back and his trusty sidekick Arjen Robben. This week, they get stuck in the Channel Tunnel.

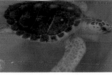

Turtle Face

7pm BBC Two

Steven Gerrard dons a green morph suit, a papier-mache shell, learns underwater-Japanese and fulfils a lifelong ambition: swimming with turtles off the North Wales coast.

Costa on the Costa

8.30pm BBC Three

This week Diego Costa joins Barry and Linda Smurthwaite, and their son Declan, on a self-catering holiday in Benidorm, on Spain's Costa Blanca.

Wreck-It Delph
★★★★★
7pm BBC One

The Aston Villa midfielder wants to be a hero, but his quest ends up creating carnage in a wacky arcade world.

FRIDAY

Colouring-In With Jackson Martinez

6am CBeebies

Crayons at the ready as we join Porto's Colombian striker for a bit of colouring fun. This week, it's Pablo Picasso's 1941 classic, Dora Maar Au Chat.

Gareth Barry Investigates

7pm BBC One

The Everton midfielder confronts a cowboy builder in Surrey – but things don't go to plan and our investigative reporter ends up in A&E.

Big Sam's Welly Wanging Festival

9pm BBC Three

Sam Allardyce returns with his annual welly boot-throwing championships, live from Bognor Regis. He has promised that, this year, no cows will be hurt.

Nani McPhee
★★ *7pm BBC One*

The erratic winger plays a child-minder in a wild household – and is forced to use his magical powers to end the chaos.

LIVE FOOTBALL

1 LIVE FA Cup
Saturday 5.35pm
BBC Sports 6

Shrewsbury host Man. City at the Greenhous Meadow in a David v Goliath clash.

2 LIVE Premier League
Sunday 1.30pm
BBC Sports 6

Louis Van Gaal takes his Man. United team to Anfield for English football's biggest match.

3 LIVE Premier League
Monday 7pm
BBC Sports 6

It's the north London derby as Arsenal take on Tottenham at White Hart Lane – you can expect plenty of fireworks.

4 LIVE Champions League
Tuesday 7.45pm
BBC Sports 6

Real Madrid and Barcelona go head-to-head at the Nou Camp.

5 LIVE Champions League
Wednesday 7.45pm
BBC Sports 6

David Luiz returns to Stamford Bridge with PSG to face off with Chelsea in this battle of the billionaires.

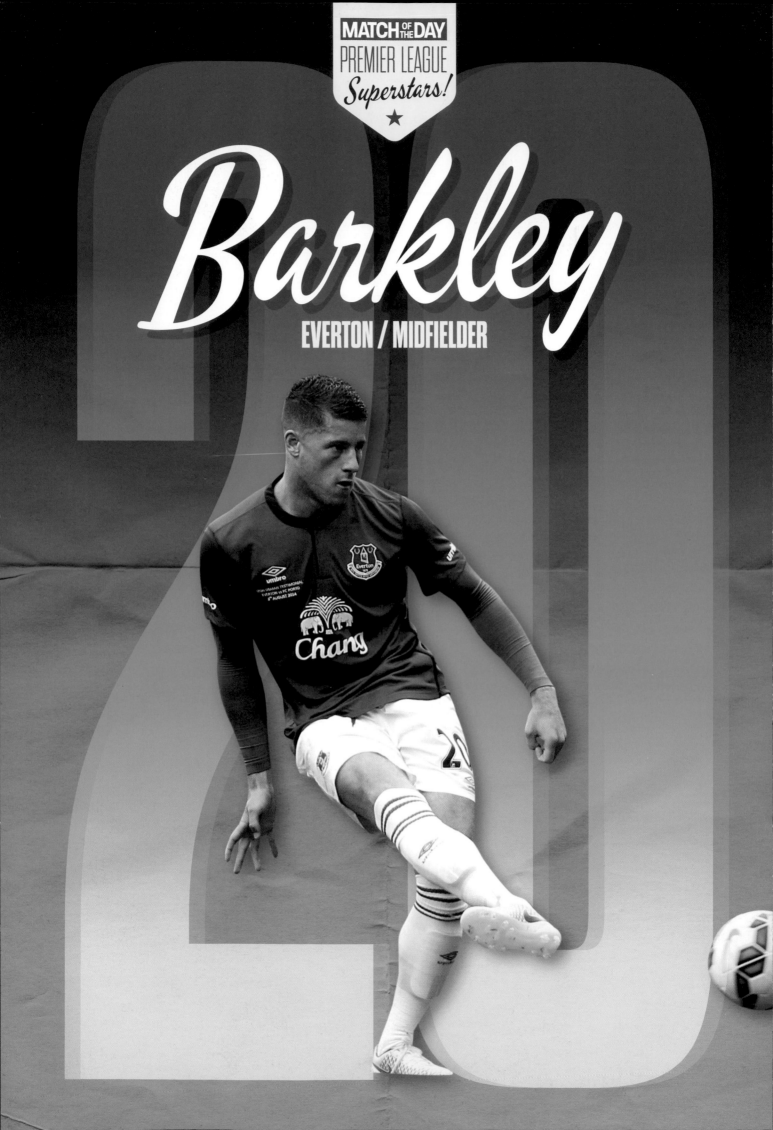

Barkley

EVERTON / MIDFIELDER

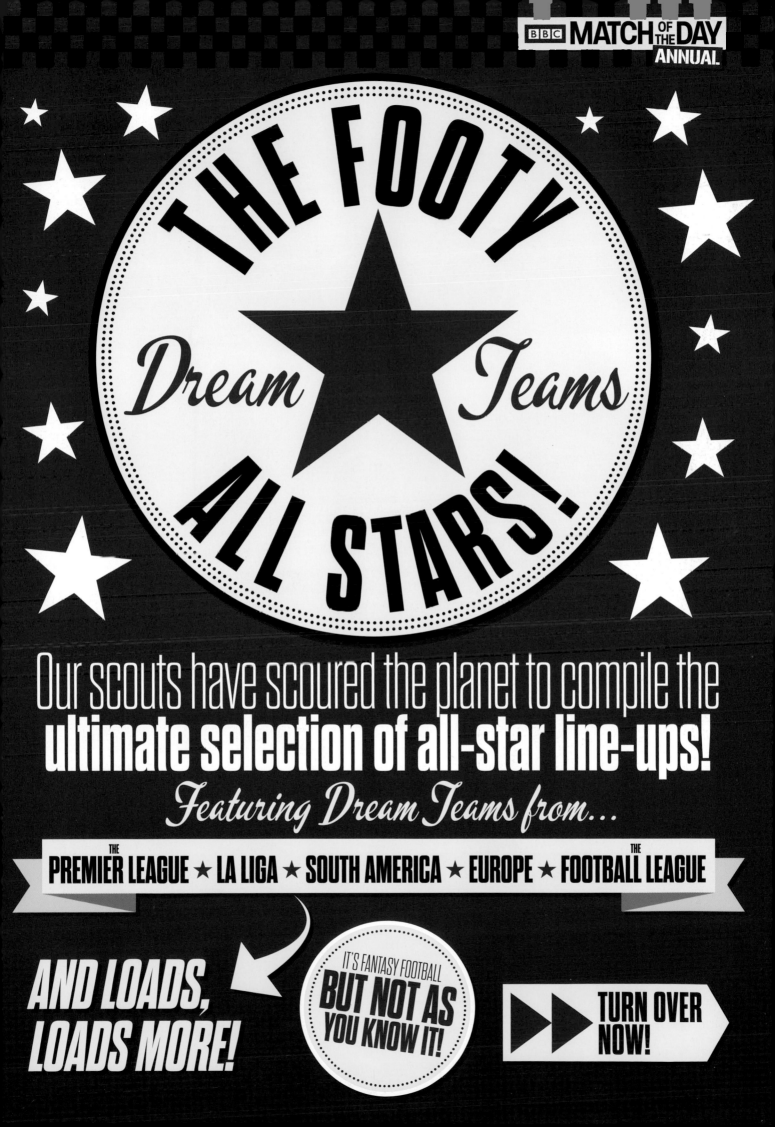

PREMIER LEAGUE

Playing style High tempo
Formation 4-4-2
Manager Jose Mourinho, Chelsea

Quality runs all the way through this awesome team with a real mix of world-class experience and a new generation of exciting talent. The pace, power and arrogance is a genuinely frightening combination!

Thibaut **COURTOIS**
CHELSEA

Pablo **ZABALETA**
MAN. CITY

Vincent **KOMPANY**
MAN. CITY

Laurent **KOSCIELNY**
ARSENAL

Leighton **BAINES**
EVERTON

Raheem **STERLING**
LIVERPOOL

Yaya **TOURE**
MAN. CITY

Cesc **FABREGAS**
CHELSEA

Eden **HAZARD**
CHELSEA

Radamel **FALCAO**
MAN. UNITED

Sergio **AGUERO**
MAN. CITY

LIGUE 1

Playing style Ultra-attacking
Formation 4-3-3
Manager Marcelo Bielsa, Marseille

Attack is the name of the game for this line-up from the French top flight. Verratti will pull the strings in midfield, whilst the PSG front three is, quite simply, a fearsome sight!

Vincent **ENYEAMA**
LILLE

Serge **AURIER**
PSG

Thiago **SILVA**
PSG

David **LUIZ**
PSG

Layvin **KURZAWA**
MONACO

Marco **VERRATTI**
PSG

Thiago **MOTTA**
PSG

Blaise **MATUIDI**
PSG

Lucas **MOURA**
PSG0

Zlatan **IBRAHIMOVIC**
PSG

Edinson **CAVANI**
PSG

SERIE A

Playing style Possession
Formation 4-3-3
Manager Rudi Garcia, Roma

That three-man midfield would strike fear into the hearts of all their opponents – we get a bit jittery just thinking about it. The South Americans up top ain't bad either!

Gianluigi **BUFFON**
JUVENTUS

MAICON
ROMA

Giorgio **CHIELLINI**
JUVENTUS

LEANDRO **CASTAN**
ROMA

Kwadwo **ASAMOAH**
JUVENTUS

Arturo **VIDAL**
JUVENTUS

Andrea **PIRLO**
JUVENTUS

Paul **POGBA**
JUVENTUS

Guillermo **CUADRADO**
FIORENTINA

Carlos **TEVEZ**
JUVENTUS

Gonzalo **HIGUAIN**
NAPOLI

BUNDESLIGA

Playing style Possession
Formation 4-2-3-1
Manager Pep Guardiola, Bayern Munich

Not so much a dream team – more a Bayern and Dortmund combo. With electric pace down the flanks, two exceptional midfielders and a clinical predator up top, it's scary!

Manuel **NEUER**
BAYERN MUNICH

Philipp **LAHM**
BAYERN MUNICH

Mats **HUMMELS**
BORUSSIA DORTMUND

Mehdi **BENATIA**
BAYERN MUNICH

David **ALABA**
BAYERN MUNICH

Bastian **SCHWEINSTEIGER**
BAYERN MUNICH

Xabi **ALONSO**
BAYERN MUNICH

Arjen **ROBBEN**
BAYERN MUNICH

Thomas **MULLER**
BAYERN MUNICH

Marco **REUS**
BORUSSIA DORTMUND

Robert **LEWANDOWSKI**
BAYERN MUNICH

LA LIGA

Playing style All-out-attack
Formation 4-1-3-2
Manager Diego Simeone, Atletico Madrid

The front five is not only worth a staggering £500 million, but it would be simply impossible for any other 11 to stop. In fact, if you were putting together a planet Earth dream team, that would be your attack right there!

Keylor **NAVAS**
REAL MADRID

Sergio **RAMOS**
REAL MADRID

Raphael **VARANE**
REAL MADRID

Diego **GODIN**
ATLETICO MADRID

Jordi **ALBA**
BARCELONA

Toni **KROOS**
REAL MADRID

Cristiano **RONALDO**
REAL MADRID

James **RODRIGUEZ**
REAL MADRID

Gareth **BALE**
REAL MADRID

Luis **SUAREZ**
BARCELONA

Lionel **MESSI**
BARCELONA

REST OF EUROPEAN LEAGUES

MLS

FOOTBALL LEAGUE

JASPER **CILLESSEN**
AJAX

DANILO
PORTO

Bruno **MARTINS INDI**
PORTO

Ezequiel **GARAY**
ZENIT

Jetro **WILLEMS**
PSV

Axel **WITSEL**
ZENIT

William **CARVALHO**
SPORTING LISBON

Ahmed **MUSA**
CSKA MOSCOW

Mathieu **VALBUENA**
DYNAMO MOSCOW

Memphis **DEPAY**
PSV

Jackson **MARTINEZ**
PORTO

Rais **MBOLHI**
PHILADELPHIA

DeAndre **YEDLIN**
SEATTLE SOUNDERS

Matt **BESLER**
KANSAS CITY

Omar **GONZALEZ**
LA GALAXY

Seth **SINOVIC**
KANSAS CITY

Kyle **BECKERMAN**
REAL SALT LAKE

Clint **DEMPSEY**
SEATTLE SOUNDERS

Tim **CAHILL**
NEW YORK RED BULLS

Landon **DONOVAN**
LA GALAXY

Thierry **HENRY**
NEW YORK RED BULLS

Bradley **WRIGHT-PHILLIPS**
NEW YORK RED BULLS

David **MARSHALL**
CARDIFF

John **BRAYFORD**
CARDIFF

Emerson **BOYCE**
WIGAN

Michael **MANCIENNE**
NOTT'M FOREST

FABIO
CARDIFF

Will **HUGHES**
DERBY

Adam **FORSHAW**
WIGAN

Craig **BRYSON**
DERBY

Callum **McMANAMAN**
WIGAN

Andy **REID**
NOTT'M FOREST

Jordan **RHODES**
BLACKBURN

SOUTH AMERICA

Playing style Attacking **Formation** 4-2-3-1
Manager Jorge Sampaoli, Chile

Good luck to any team facing this lot! The creativity and goalscoring power in attack is just mind-blowing – and the bite and tenacity in midfield means the opposition attackers are not going to get a kick against them!

Claudio **BRAVO**
CHILE

Pablo **ZABALETA**
ARGENTINA

Diego **GODIN**
URUGUAY

Thiago **SILVA**
BRAZIL

MARCELO
BRAZIL

Arturo **VIDAL**
CHILE

Javier **MASCHERANO**
ARGENTINA

Lionel **MESSI**
ARGENTINA

James **RODRIGUEZ**
COLOMBIA

NEYMAR
BRAZIL

Luis **SUAREZ**
URUGUAY

AFRICA

Playing style Positive **Formation** 4-4-2
Manager Stephen Keshi, Nigeria

The African nations may not have lit up the World Cup, but this line-up would give anyone problems. An incredible shot-stopper, wicked attacking full-backs, pace out wide, quality up front and Yaya Toure bossing it in midfield!

Vincent **ENYEAMA**
NIGERIA

Serge **AURIER**
IVORY COAST

Mehdi **BENATIA**
MOROCCO

Joel **MATIP**
CAMEROON

Kwadwo **ASAMOAH**
GHANA

Ahmed **MUSA**
NIGERIA

Yaya **TOURE**
IVORY COAST

Ogenyi **ONAZI**
NIGERIA

Sofiane **FEGHOULI**
ALGERIA

Asamoah **GYAN**
GHANA

Pierre-Emerick **AUBAMEYANG**
GABON

ASIA

Playing style High-tempo **Formation** 4-2-3-1
Manager Javier Aguirre, Japan

Unsurprisingly, Japan and South Korea provide the bulk of this team. They'll look to keep the ball, play neat little passes before using the creativity of Shinji Kagawa and Keisuke Honda to release the explosive Son Heung-Min!

Ali **AL-HABSI**
OMAN

Atsuto **UCHIDA**
JAPAN

Maya **YOSHIDA**
JAPAN

KIM Young-Gwon
SOUTH KOREA

Yuto **NAGATOMO**
JAPAN

Makoto **HASEBE**
JAPAN

Ki SUNG-YEUNG
SOUTH KOREA

Ashkan **DEJAGAH**
IRAN

Keisuke **HONDA**
JAPAN

Shinji **KAGAWA**
JAPAN

SON Heung-Min
SOUTH KOREA

EUROPE

Playing style Passing
Formation 4-3-3
Manager Joachim Low, Germany

Most teams have some kind of weakness – but if you can spot one in this line-up let us know. It's dripping with world-class ability from the big German keeper all the way through to the man known simply as Zlatan!

Manuel **NEUER** — GERMANY

Philipp **LAHM** — GERMANY
Vincent **KOMPANY** — BELGIUM
Raphael **VARANE** — FRANCE
David **ALABA** — AUSTRIA

Paul **POGBA** — FRANCE
Andrea **PIRLO** — ITALY
Toni **KROOS** — GERMANY

Cristiano **RONALDO** — PORTUGAL
Gareth **BALE** — WALES
Zlatan **IBRAHIMOVIC** — SWEDEN

NORTH & CENTRAL AMERICA

Playing style Energetic **Formation** 4-3-2-1
Manager Jurgen Klinsmann, USA

The Brazil 2014 World Cup proved to be a real platform for the CONCACAF nations – with unknowns exploding onto the world stage. The energy, desire and technique of these stars now matches any other region in the world!

Keylor **NAVAS** — COSTA RICA

Fabian **JOHNSON** — USA
Matt **BESLER** — USA
Giancarlo **GONZALEZ** — COSTA RICA
Junior **DIAZ** — COSTA RICA

DeAndre **YEDLIN** — USA
Hector **HERRERA** — MEXICO
Andres **GUARDADO** — MEXICO

Clint **DEMPSEY** — USA
Celso **BORGES** — COSTA RICA

Javier **HERNANDEZ** — MEXICO

2014 WORLD CUP

Playing style Attacking **Formation** 4-1-3-2
Manager Louis Van Gaal, Holland

How do you squeeze all of the summer's attacking talent into one team? It's been tough and some household names have missed out – but if you were to send this lot into battle, you'd be guaranteed goals and a big victory!

Manuel **NEUER** — GERMANY

Philipp **LAHM** — GERMANY
Thiago **SILVA** — BRAZIL
Ron **VLAAR** — HOLLAND
Daley **BLIND** — HOLLAND

Javier **MASCHERANO** — ARGENTINA

Arjen **ROBBEN** — HOLLAND
James **RODRIGUEZ** — COLOMBIA
NEYMAR — BRAZIL

Lionel **MESSI** — ARGENTINA
Thomas **MULLER** — GERMANY

ALL-TIME WORLD

Playing style Showboating **Formation** 4-3-1-2
Manager Sir Alex Ferguson, 1974-2013

You just have to take a deep breath and sit down when you imagine what these 11 legends would be able to produce if they were ever magically brought together to play in the same team!

Lev **YASHIN**
SOVIET UNION

CAFU BRAZIL
Franz **BECKENBAUER** WEST GERMANY
Franco **BARESI** ITALY
Giacinto **FACHETTI** ITALY

Johan **CRUYFF** HOLLAND
Alfredo **DI STEFANO** ARGENTINA/SPAIN
Zindine **ZIDANE** FRANCE

Diego **MARADONA** ARGENTINA

Lionel **MESSI** ARGENTINA
PELE BRAZIL

ALL-TIME ENGLAND

Playing style High tempo **Formation** 4-2-3-1
Manager Sir Alf Ramsey, 1963-74

With almost 1,000 caps between them you're looking at 11 huge legends of English football. This truly is the best of the hundreds of players who've pulled on the England jersey!

Gordon **BANKS**
73 CAPS

Gary **Neville** 85 CAPS
Bobby **MOORE** 108 CAPS
Billy **WRIGHT** 105 CAPS
Ashley **COLE** 107 CAPS

Bryan **ROBSON** 90 CAPS
Paul **GASCOIGNE** 57 CAPS

Stanley **MATTHEWS** 90 CAPS
Bobby **CHARLTON** 106 CAPS
Tom **FINNEY** 76 CAPS

Gary **LINEKER** 80 CAPS

2018 WORLD CUP

Playing style Attacking **Formation:** 4-1-4-1
Manager Jogi Low, Germany

These are the lads who will write their name into World Cup history in four years' time. They're stars already – but when it comes to Russia 2018, they'll be full-blown superstars!

Thibaut **COURTOIS**
BELGIUM

Serge **AURIER** IVORY COAST
Raphael **VARANE** FRANCE
MARQUINHOS BRAZIL
Luke **SHAW** ENGLAND

Paul **POGBA** FRANCE

Raheem **STERLING** ENGLAND
James **RODRIGUEZ** COLOMBIA
Julian **DRAXLER** GERMANY
Adnan **JANUZAJ** BELGIUM

NEYMAR BRAZIL

PAZ'S FAVOURITE ALL-TIME

Neville **SOUTHALL**

Philipp **LAHM**
Rio **FERDINAND**
Franco **BARESI**
Paolo **MALDINI**

Paul **SCHOLES**
XAVI

Victor **KASULE**
Dragan **STOIJKOVIC**
Zinedine **ZIDANE**

ROMARIO

BEZ'S FAVOURITE ALL-TIME

Gianluigi **BUFFON**

Lilian **THURAM**
Franco **BARESI**
Sol **CAMPBELL**
Steve **GUPPY**

Chris **BART-WILLIAMS**
Roy **KEANE**

Zinedine **ZIDANE**

Dennis **BERGKAMP**
Scott **McGLEISH**
Thierry **HENRY**

NOW IT'S YOUR TURN!

MY CURRENT ALL-STAR LINE-UP!

WHICH OF TODAY'S WORLD STARS WILL MAKE YOUR DREAM TEAM?

Design your team's kit!

Keeper
Centre-back
Centre-back
Right-back
Left-back
Midfielder
Midfielder
INIESTA
Midfielder
ZIDANE
Forward
MARADONA
Striker
MESSI
Forward
PELE

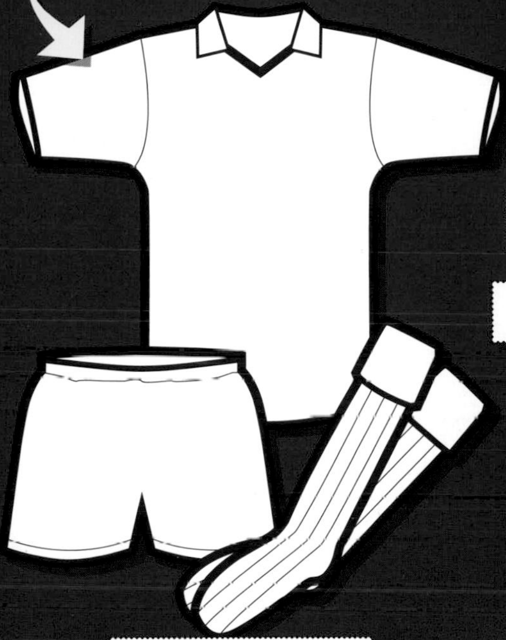

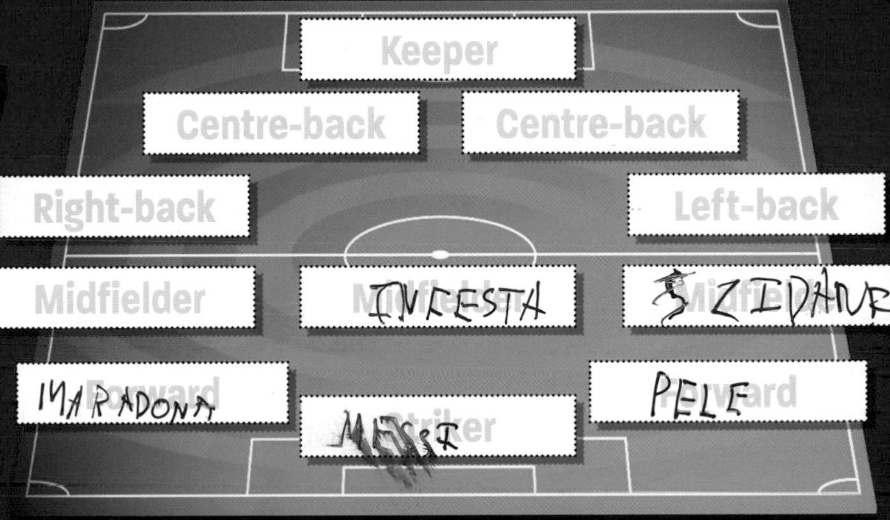

TEAM NAME

STADIUM NAME NOU CAMP

MANAGER

MY SCHOOL / JUNIOR TEAM!

Design your team's kit!

Keeper
Centre-back
Centre-back
Right-back
Left-back
Midfielder
Midfielder
Midfielder
Forward
Striker
Forward

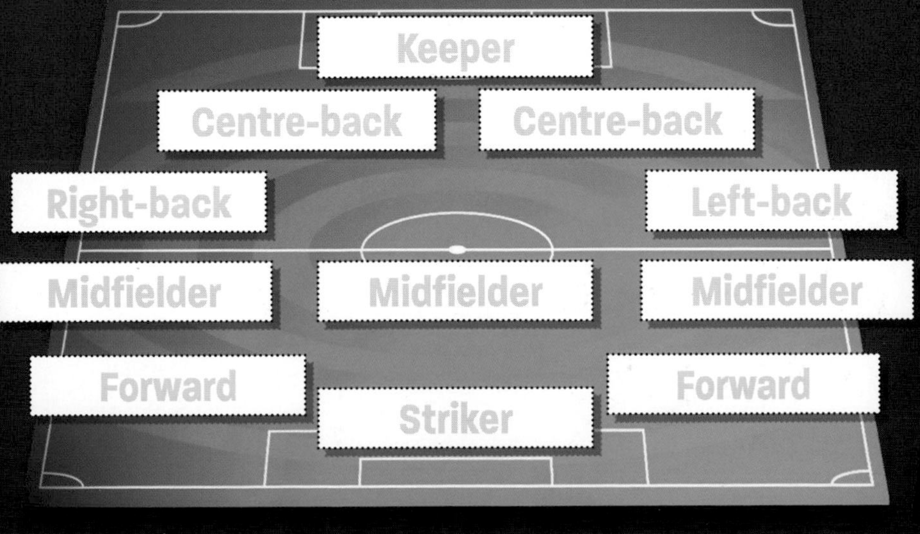

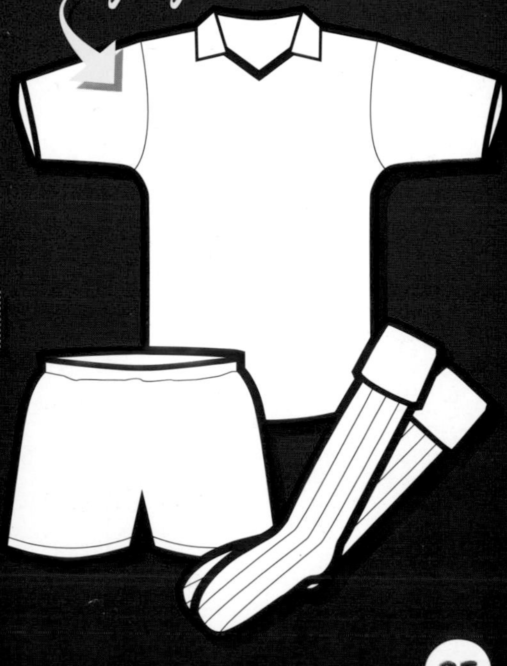

TEAM NAME

MANAGER

WHICH FOREIGN TEA

Not sure? Just answer the questions i

START HERE!

Do you like football? → **YES**

NO

We mean real football, not American football → **YES** → Yeah, that's me

OH

Put this book down and walk away

You must be a robot ← **NO** ← Do you eat food? → **YES**

Sausages

What's your favourite?

Steak

Slapped on a BBQ

With chips and a tasty sauce

Do you like to follow the crowd? ← Yeah, it's not a bad thing

He's not as good as Maradona

Is Pele a legend?

YOU SHOULD SUPPORT

Even if it means not winning the league?

I like to be different

FLAMENGO

Yeah, history is way more important

YOU SHOULD SUPPORT

CABJ

BOCA JUNIORS

Yep, total ledge!

YOU SHOULD SUPPORT

S.F.C.

SANTOS

YES ← But you like cool kits?

YOU SHOULD SUPPORT

SAINT-ETIENNE A.S.S.E LOIRE

SAINT ETIENNE

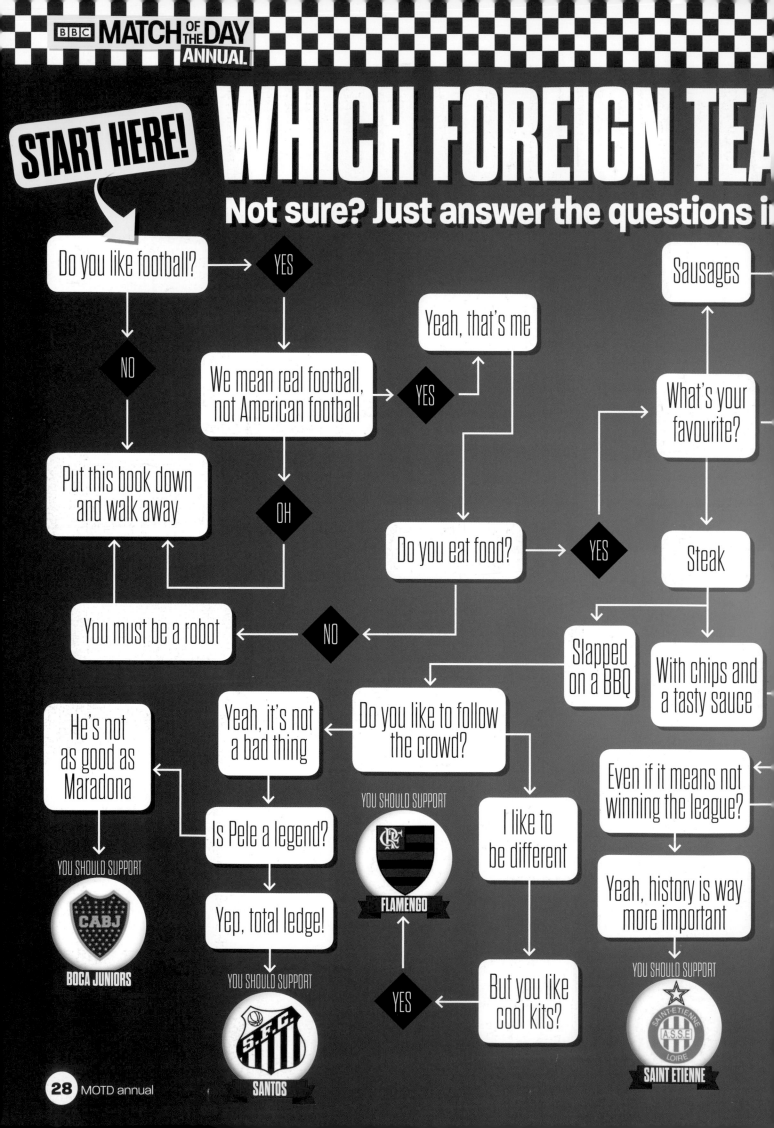

M SHOULD YOU SUPPORT?

ur wicked flow chart and you'll find out!

Big tasty bangers?

Yeah! Yum Yum!

I live for success — nothing else matters

YOU SHOULD SUPPORT

BAYERN MUNICH

I prefer chorizo

How important is winning to you?

It's nice — but I'd rather people think I'm cool

Cheese

And ham?

I'm more flip-flops and shorts

And you love iconic stadiums, yeah?

But still with the chance of winning trophies?

NO

YES

Stylish trainers and jeans?

YOU SHOULD SUPPORT

BARCELONA

YES

Is tradition important?

YOU SHOULD SUPPORT

ATLETICO MADRID

NO

YES

Do you love an underdog?

YES

YES

Actually, probably not

I'm only interested in having loads of cash and world-class players

NO

Nah, it's all about being a superpower

YOU SHOULD SUPPORT

BORUSSIA DORTMUND

Not as cool as hanging out with Mickey Mouse at Disneyland

How does sun, sea and expensive yachts sound?

YOU SHOULD SUPPORT

REAL MADRID

I don't care as long as I stand out from the crowd

YOU SHOULD SUPPORT

PSG

Wicked!

YOU SHOULD SUPPORT

MONACO

YOU SHOULD SUPPORT

ST PAULI

50/ELFTY

1 WHO'S FASTER?

GET THE ANSWERS ON p92!

A Cristiano Ronaldo

B A cheetah ✓

2 WHO'S OLDER?

A Arsene Wenger

B The Queen ✓

3 WHO'S TALLER?

A Three Peter Crouchs on top of each other ✓

B A double-decker bus

4 WHAT'S BEEN AROUND LONGER?

A Southampton's St Mary's Stadium

B EastEnders ✓

5 WHICH WEIGHS MORE?

A Kumbuka the gorilla from London Zoo ✓

B Sergio Aguero and Alvaro Negredo together

6 WHICH IS LONGER?

A A football pitch

B The Eiffel Tower lying down ✓

7 WHICH COST MORE TO MAKE?

A Wembley Stadium ✓

B Despicable Me 2

8 WHO'S SCORED MORE GOALS?

A Wayne Rooney ✓

B Mr Bean

▶▶▶ TURN TO PAGE 34 FOR MORE QUIZ ACTION!

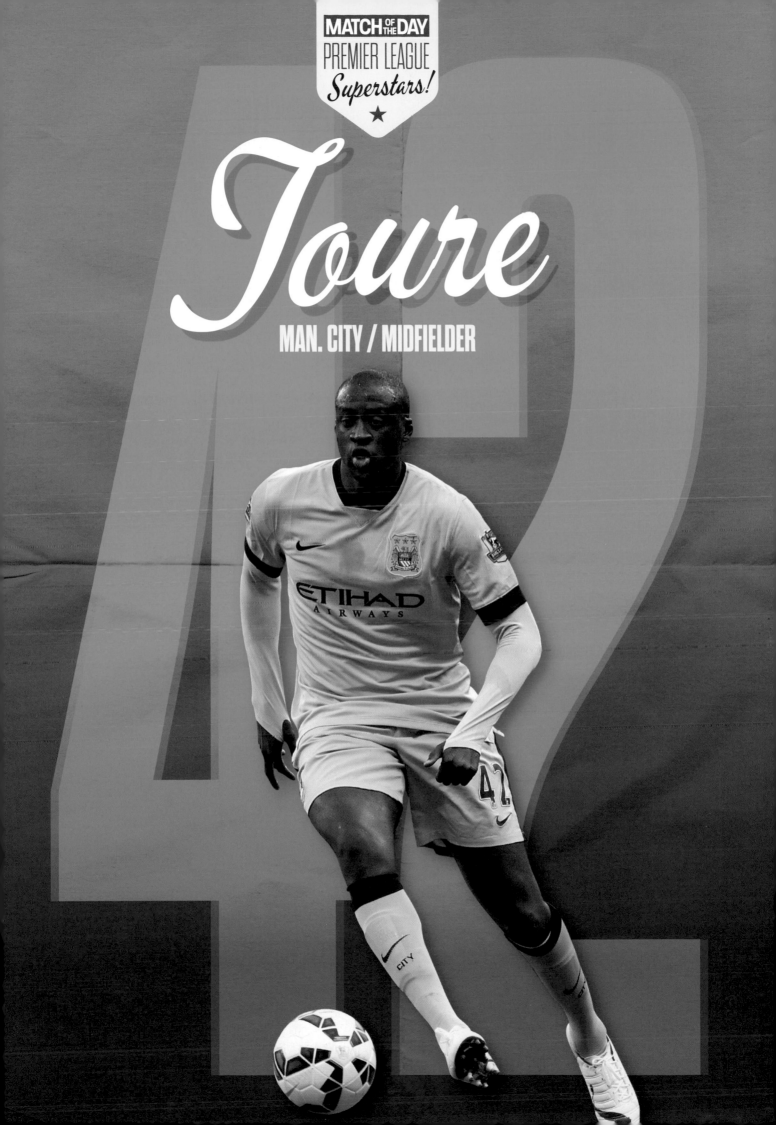

DiMaria

MAN. UNITED / MIDFIELDER

THE WORLD CUP OF STUPID BADGES!

There's a whole world of utterly bonkers footy badges out there – but which one is the weirdest? Let's find out by putting them head-to-head in a classic knockout!

QUARTER-FINALS!

CALAIS RACING UNION
FRANCE

V

HOME FARM
REPUBLIC OF IRELAND

A man in a yellow trackie feeding some fish – how can that fail to win? When it's up against a football with red hair and clown shoes, that's when!

WINNER CALAIS RACING UNION

ROI ET UNITED
THAILAND

V

VV NOORDWIJK
HOLLAND

The feisty little squirrel – that looks like Alvin the chipmunk – is no match for the weird blue thing. Is it a tadpole? An alien? Dunno!

WINNER VV NOORDWIJK

BRASILIENSE FC
BRAZIL

V

ESPERANCE DE TUNIS
TUNISIA

Why would you stick a cartoon croc on your badge, even if he's all smiley? But that's still not as weird as a daft-looking, fez-wearing Tunisian school kid!

WINNER ESPERANCE DE TUNIS

CHANGCHUN YATAI
CHINA

V

ARAGUAINA
ARGENTINA

You shouldn't use photos on a badge – especially a photo of a cow. But, at least you can tell it's a cow. That Chinese pig-deer-duck thing is far, far too creepy!

WINNER CHANGCHUN YATAI

SEMI-FINALS!

CALAIS RACING UNION
FRANCE

V

VV NOORDWIJK
HOLLAND

It's a semi-final clash between two lower-league European clubs. Noordwijk's blue blob does confuse us, but in terms of laugh-out-loud stupid, it's not a patch on Calais' ball-head!

WINNER CALAIS RACING UNION

ESPERANCE DE TUNIS
TUNISIA

V

CHANGCHUN YATAI
CHINA

Esperance are Tunisian champs and Changchun play in the Chinese top flight, so their odd badges surprise us. Once again, the creepiness of the duck-creature takes the spoils!

WINNER CHANGCHUN YATAI

FINAL!

CALAIS RACING UNION
FRANCE

CHANGCHUN YATAI
CHINA

Stupidest badge!

We've reached the final! It's Calais' best cup run since they were shock finalists in the French Cup 14 years ago – and while both badges are proper weird, the ball with the wig and big clown feet does enough to secure a massive win for the French outfit. Allez Calais!

WINNER CALAIS RACING UNION

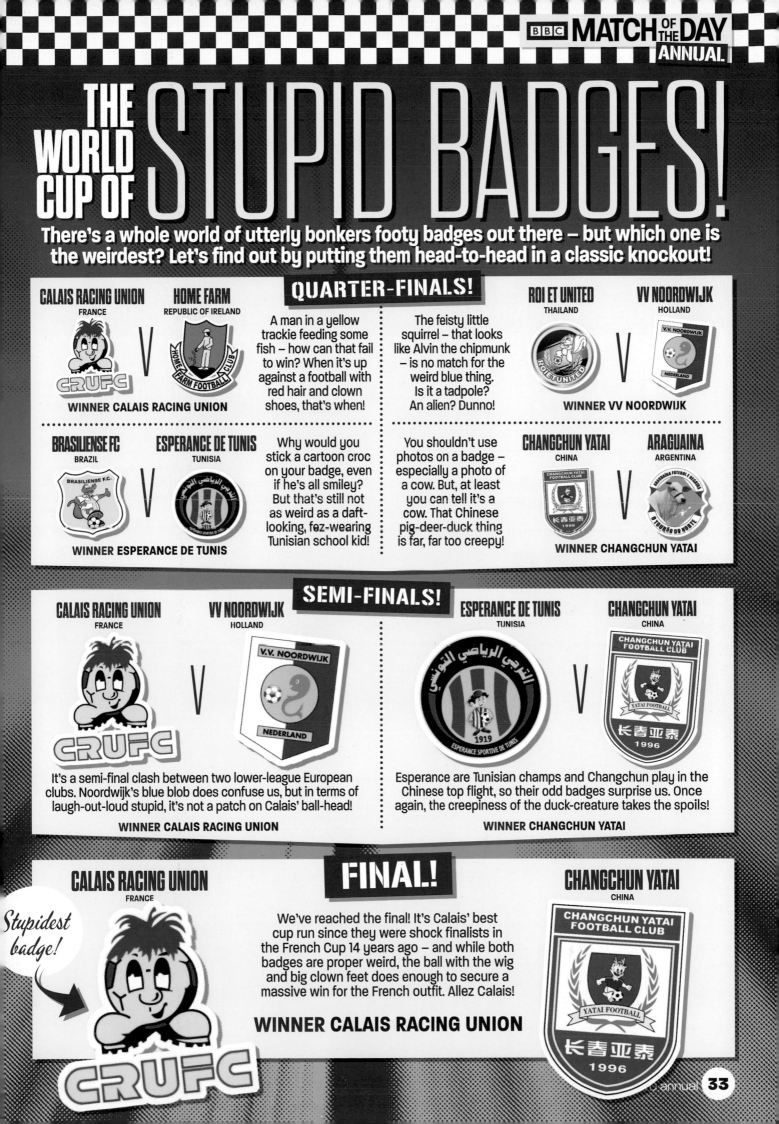

MIDDLE-NAME CONFESSIONS!

Guess which middle name belongs to each player!

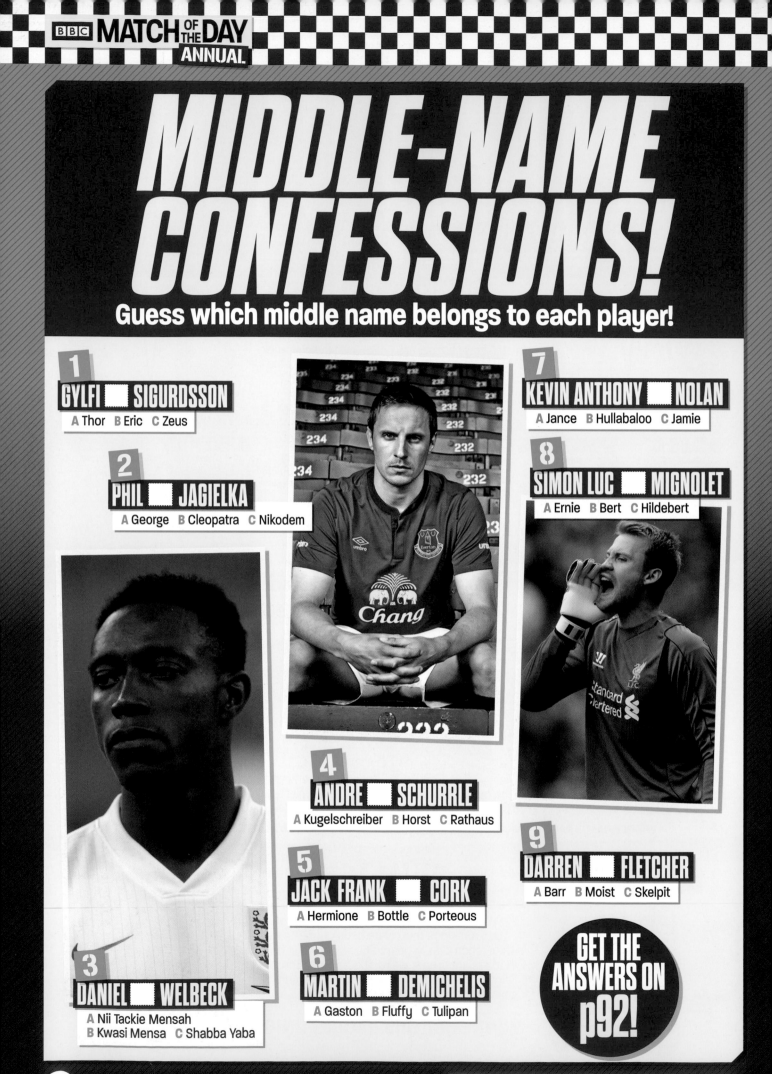

1 GYLFI ☐ SIGURDSSON
A Thor B Eric C Zeus

2 PHIL ☐ JAGIELKA
A George B Cleopatra C Nikodem

3 DANIEL ☐ WELBECK
A Nii Tackie Mensah
B Kwasi Mensa C Shabba Yaba

4 ANDRE ☐ SCHURRLE
A Kugelschreiber B Horst C Rathaus

5 JACK FRANK ☐ CORK
A Hermione B Bottle C Porteous

6 MARTIN ☐ DEMICHELIS
A Gaston B Fluffy C Tulipan

7 KEVIN ANTHONY ☐ NOLAN
A Jance B Hullabaloo C Jamie

8 SIMON LUC ☐ MIGNOLET
A Ernie B Bert C Hildebert

9 DARREN ☐ FLETCHER
A Barr B Moist C Skelpit

GET THE ANSWERS ON p92!

▶▶▶ TURN TO PAGE 42 FOR MORE QUIZ ACTION!

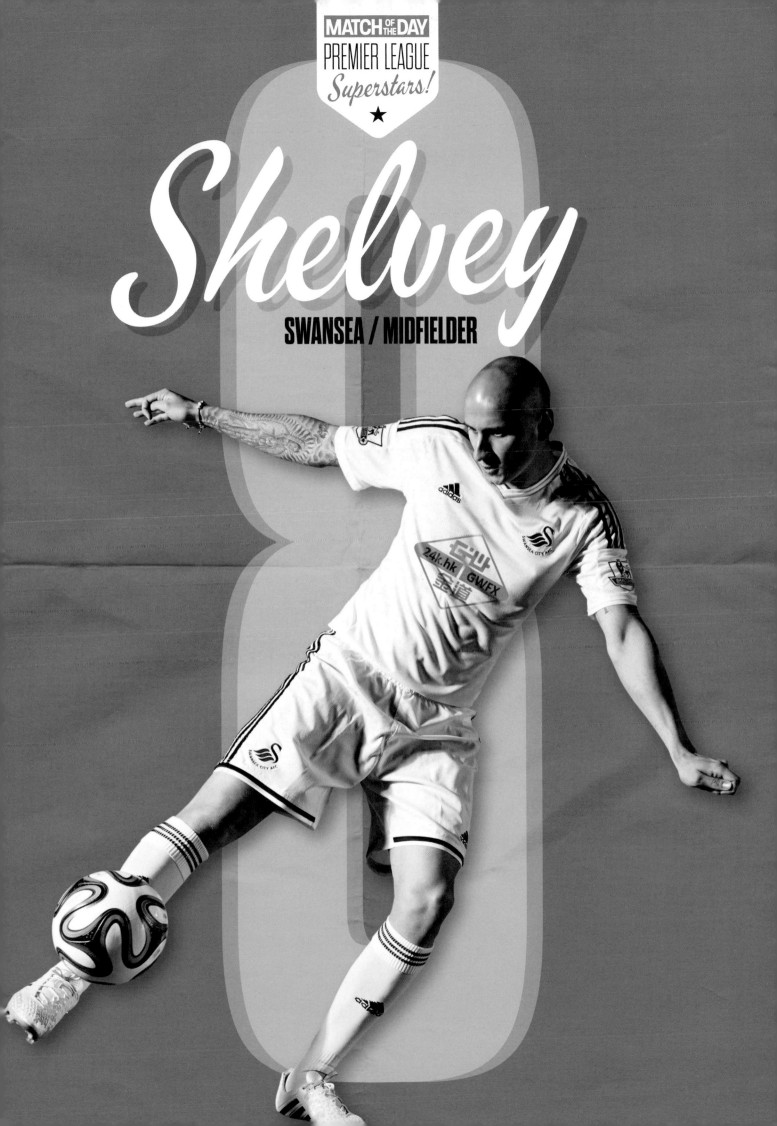

SHOOT!

"He's gonna hit it, you know!"

MOTD reveals the ten most trigger-happy strikers in the Prem!

▶▶▶ **TURN OVER TO SEE WHO'S IN OUR TOP 10!**

10 JAY RODRIGUEZ
SOUTHAMPTON

71.5
Shots per season!

Southampton fans have got used to this guy lining one up. Jay's shooting boots racked up 15 goals for The Saints last season and led to his first ever England call-up. He doesn't often leather it, but instead prefers to rely on the measured placement of his smooth right foot!

9 DANIEL STURRIDGE
LIVERPOOL

73
Shots per season!

Where Daniel Sturridge's shots go, his funny little jive-dance normally follows. He's become one of THE deadliest marksmen in the Premier League in recent years and no wonder – last season it took him just three-and-a-half swishes of his left foot to find the back of the net!

8 ROMELU LUKAKU
EVERTON

Lukaku takes the title for the league's most accurate striker – last season he hit the target with 69% of his shots and more than a quarter of those went in. He's yet to break the 20-goal barrier in the Prem, but with stats like that this could be the season!

77
Shots per season!

7 EDIN DZEKO
MAN. CITY

Dzeko is one of the most two-footed strikers on our list. Last season, his shots on target were split pretty evenly between his left and right foot, and don't even get us started on his heading. The 28-year-old's aerial ability makes him one of the Prem's most complete strikers!

79.5
Shots per season!

6 RICKIE LAMBERT
LIVERPOOL

80
Shots per season!

If he packed beetroot in his factory days half as quickly as he gets shots off in England's top flight, he must have been a highly efficient worker. Lambert looks like a centre-half, but in fact he has the left foot of a wizard and is an expert at making space for himself to let rip!

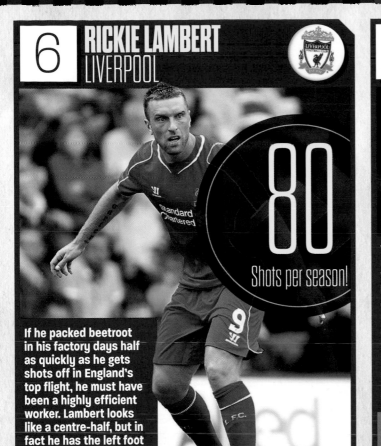

5 SERGIO AGUERO
MAN. CITY

The Aguero piledriver really is a thing of beauty. Two seasons ago he lashed one into the roof of the net against Man. United at Old Trafford, and that stands out for us as our favourite Sergio shot since he moved to England in 2011. We'll have more of the same this term please, mate!

80.3
Shots per season!

4 OLIVIER GIROUD
ARSENAL

Call him Mr Consistent – Giroud has hit the same number of shots (88) for the last two seasons running. If we had to put money on it we'd say the majority of those came inside the box, at the near post – a textbook Giroud finish!

88
Shots per season!

▶▶▶ **TURN OVER TO SEE WHO'S No.1!**

TOP TOTS!

Guess which top Prem stars and managers we've pictured here with baby heads!

GET THE ANSWERS ON p92!

1 ANSWER

2 ANSWER

3 ANSWER

4 ANSWER

5 ANSWER

6 ANSWER

▶▶▶ TURN TO p66 FOR MORE QUIZ ACTION!

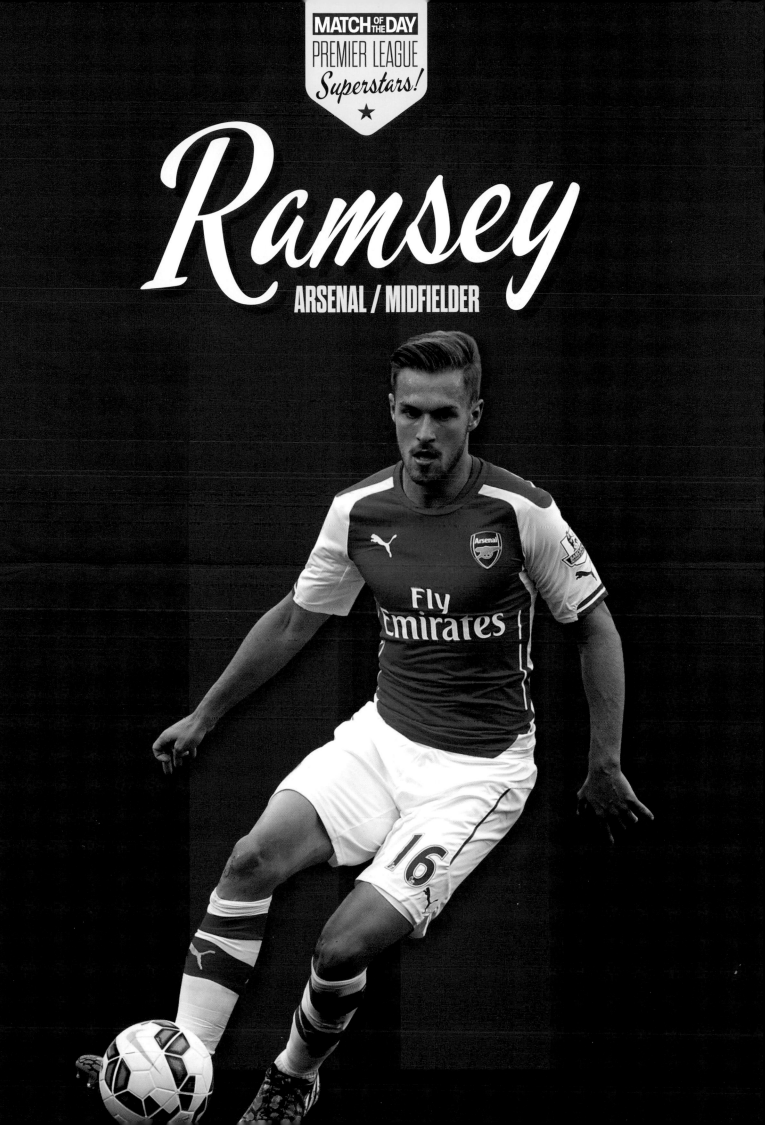

The RISE of RAHEEM

20 YEARS THAT CREATED A SUPERSTAR!

1994
Raheem first popped his little head into the world in Kingston, Jamaica way back in 1994!

1999
At the age of five, Raheem's mum upped sticks to north-west London – right near Wembley stadium!

2004
Five years later, Raheem got his first taste of pro football when he was spotted by QPR's academy!

2009
After signing for QPR he created quite a stir – before long he was called up to the England Under-16s!

2010
His England exposure set the wheels in motion for a big move – Prem giants Chelsea and Man. United were both interested, but Liverpool won the race!

> "I grew up five minutes from Wembley. I'm really grateful to get the opportunity to play there!"

2012
On 24 March 2012, then boss Kenny Dalglish handed Sterling his professional debut against Wigan, making him Liverpool's second-youngest player of all time. Pretty impressive stuff!

It was Brendan Rodgers who gave him his first start the following term in a 2-2 draw with Man. City. He went on to play 24 Prem games that season!

Just a month later, in September 2012, Roy Hodgson noticed his potential and called him up to the full England squad for the first time!

He had to wait until the November friendly with Sweden to play though – England lost 4-2 but a new international career was born!

2013
By the start of the 2013-14 season, the journey from zero to hero was complete – Sterling started the campaign as a key member of the Liverpool starting 11!

2014
The icing on the cake of a wicked season came as Sterling made it into England's World Cup squad and put in a sick display against Italy in the opening game!

WHAT THEY SAY...
about Sterling!

"Raheem's incredible rise will have taken nobody at QPR by surprise and he undoubtedly has the potential to become one of the best players in the world!"
KEVIN GALLEN
His old youth team coach at QPR

"To me, he's my little brother and I look after him and try to help him as a footballer and as a person!"
DANIEL STURRIDGE
Liverpool team-mate

"If Sterling gives himself the best chance to succeed, he could be absolutely anything he wants to be. He's a very special talent!"
GARY LINEKER
MOTD presenter

"If you saw him training you will have seen some outstanding moments. Some of the things he does out there are breathtaking!"
ROY HODGSON
England manager

"He is the toughest in our squad. I don't go near him in training because if I do, there is only one winner!"
STEVEN GERRARD
Liverpool captain

▶▶▶ **TURN OVER FOR MORE RAHEEM!**

OCTOBER 2012

I'M OFF THE MARK!
Liverpool 1-0 Reading
You could tell by the way Raheem took his first goal for Liverpool against Reading that he was going to be a big deal. The poise and precision he showed at speed, having been set free by Luis Suarez was phenomenal!

MARCH 2014

RUNNING THIS THING!
Man. United 0-3 Liverpool
This was the game when people realised Raheem was more than just a flying winger. He wasn't on the scoresheet, but he ran the midfield with his pass-and-move football – United couldn't handle him!

5 RAHEEM RIPPERS
THAT PROVED HE'S BIG TIME!

FEBRUARY 2014

I'M GUNNER GET YOU, BOYS!
Liverpool 5-1 Arsenal
Sterling's pace and link-up play had Arsenal on the ropes for long periods in the 5-1 thrashing in February, but it was his composed finishing that saw them off with two lethal strikes!

APRIL 2014

SEE YA, VINNIE!
Liverpool 3-2 Man. City
Vincent Kompany had been the best defender in the Prem for the past three seasons, but Sterling tormented him in this classic 3-2 win at Anfield!

TEENAGE TEARAWAYS!

THIS LOT ALL MADE IT BIG BEFORE THEY WERE 20 YEARS OLD!

WAYNE ROONEY
Pro debut: 16 years, 315 days
Made his Everton debut against Spurs, but it was a sick solo goal against Arsenal, ending their 30-match unbeaten run, which put him on the map!

THEO WALCOTT
Pro debut: 16 years, 143 days
Within a few months of making his Southampton debut in the Championship, Arsenal had seen enough to part with £12 million for Walcott!

MICHAEL OWEN
Pro debut: 17 years, 143 days
Owen had a reputation as a prolific goalscorer as a kid so it was no surprise when he scored the first of 222 career goals on his debut at Wimbledon!

LIONEL MESSI
Pro debut: 17 years, 114 days
Messi was one of the most talked-about teenagers in history – everybody seemed to know he was going to be a superstar and he hasn't disappointed!

CESC FABREGAS
Pro debut: 16 years, 177 days
People thought Arsene Wenger was nuts when he replaced club legend Patrick Vieira with Cesc, but he's gone on to become one of the world's best!

JUNE 2014

WORLD, HERE I COME!
England 1-2 Italy
The nation was nervous as to how he'd react to his first World Cup game against the superpower of Italy – we needn't have worried! Raheem's pace, smart passing and trickery showed he's ready to become a global star in 2015!

MOTD STAT
Raheem scored nine goals and bagged four assists in the Prem last season!

CELTIC
SCOTTISH PREMIERSHIP CHAMPIONS

MAN. CITY
PREMIER LEAGUE CHAMPIONS

2013-14 LEAGUE

ATLETICO MADRID
LA LIGA CHAMPIONS

JUVENTUS CAMPIONE D'ITALIA 2013-2014

JUVENTUS
SERIE A CHAMPIONS

PSG
LIGUE 1 CHAMPIONS

WINNERS

Thank you
#YouAreFootball

BAYERN MUNICH
BUNDESLIGA CHAMPIONS

51. DEUTSCHER MEISTER
SAISON 2013/14

Coutinho

LIVERPOOL / MIDFIELDER

33

THINGS TO DO IN

2015

Your mission, if you choose to accept it, is to complete all of these challenges in the next 12 months!

- ☑ BECOME A GENIUS!
- ☑ BECOME A SELFIE SUPERFAN!
- ☑ BECOME A LEGEND!
- ☑ BECOME AN ENTERTAINER!

►►► TURN OVER TO START!

BECOME A LEGEND!

1 Bag a hat-trick — then keep the match ball!

MISSION COMPLETED! ✔

2 Make up a celebration with your mates!

MISSION COMPLETED! ✔

3 Curl a free-kick into the top corner!

MISSION COMPLETED! ✔

Lob the keeper from outside the area!

4

MISSION COMPLETED! ✔

Pull off 100 keepy-uppies — and throw in a few cheeky ones!

5

MISSION COMPLETED! ✔

6 Nail the Cruyff Turn — and use it in a match!

MISSION COMPLETED! ✔

BECOME AN ENTERTAINER!

7 Beat the keeper with a wicked overhead kick!

MISSION COMPLETED! ✓

8 Smash an unstoppable volley off the underside of the bar!

MISSION COMPLETED! ✓

9 Score a world-class diving header!

MISSION COMPLETED! ✓

10 Learn a sick new trick every month!

MISSION COMPLETED! ✓

11 Eat an egg dressed as Marouane Fellaini!

MISSION COMPLETED! ✓

12 Get a pet hamster and name it after a Brazilian footballer!

MISSION COMPLETED! ✓

13 Design a wacky new kit for your club!

MISSION COMPLETED! ✓

14 Apply for a manager's position at a Football League club!

MISSION COMPLETED! ✓

15 Every time you see a cat, point at it and chant: 'Who are ya, who are ya?'

MISSION COMPLETED! ✓

16 Complete this story in 200 words: Lionel Messi got the fright of his life when a little green alien crash-landed in his garden. But it was soon to get even scarier for the Barcelona star because...

MISSION COMPLETED! ✓

17 Draw a picture of Steven Gerrard being fouled by Homer Simpson!

MISSION COMPLETED! ✓

▶▶▶ TURN OVER FOR MORE!

BECOME A SELFIE SUPERFAN!

18 Take a selfie at a Prem stadium!

Print it off and stick it here!

MISSION COMPLETED!

19 Take a selfie at a Football League ground!

Print it off and stick it here!

MISSION COMPLETED!

20 Take a selfie at a European stadium!

Print it off and stick it here!

MISSION COMPLETED!

21 Take a selfie at a non-league ground!

Print it off and stick it here!

MISSION COMPLETED!

22 Take a selfie with a Prem footballer!

Print it off and stick it here!

MISSION COMPLETED!

23 Take a selfie wearing a foreign footy shirt!

Print it off and stick it here!

MISSION COMPLETED!

24 Take a selfie at Wembley stadium!

Print it off and stick it here!

MISSION COMPLETED!

25 Take a selfie with your best mate — in your fave footy kits!

Print it off and stick it here!

MISSION COMPLETED!

BBC MATCH OF THE DAY ANNUAL

26 Memorise all Prem, Champo League & FA Cup winners since 1992!

MISSION COMPLETED! ✓

27 Learn every World Cup winner and host country!

MISSION COMPLETED! ✓

28 Find out who your club's record goalscorer is!

MISSION COMPLETED! ✓

29 Learn the name of every Premier League club's stadium!

MISSION COMPLETED! ✓

30 Learn the nickname of every Football League club!

MISSION COMPLETED! ✓

THE FOOTBALL LEAGUE ™

31 Understand the difference between a direct free-kick and an indirect free-kick!

MISSION COMPLETED! ✓

32 Learn 'I love football' in different languages!

French	ANSWER
Spanish	ANSWER
German	ANSWER
Italian	ANSWER

MISSION COMPLETED! ✓

33 And finally, the most important of all: PLAY FOOTBALL AT LEAST TWICE A WEEK!

How many missions did you complete?

0 Go and sit in the corner and think long and hard about what you've done!

1-9 You know that's a pretty poor effort. Big improvement needed!

10-19 Solid, if not spectacular. You can be proud of your achievement!

20-29 Now we're talking. That's a superb performance — take a bow!

29-33 All hail the football king! That sir, is a truly world-class display!

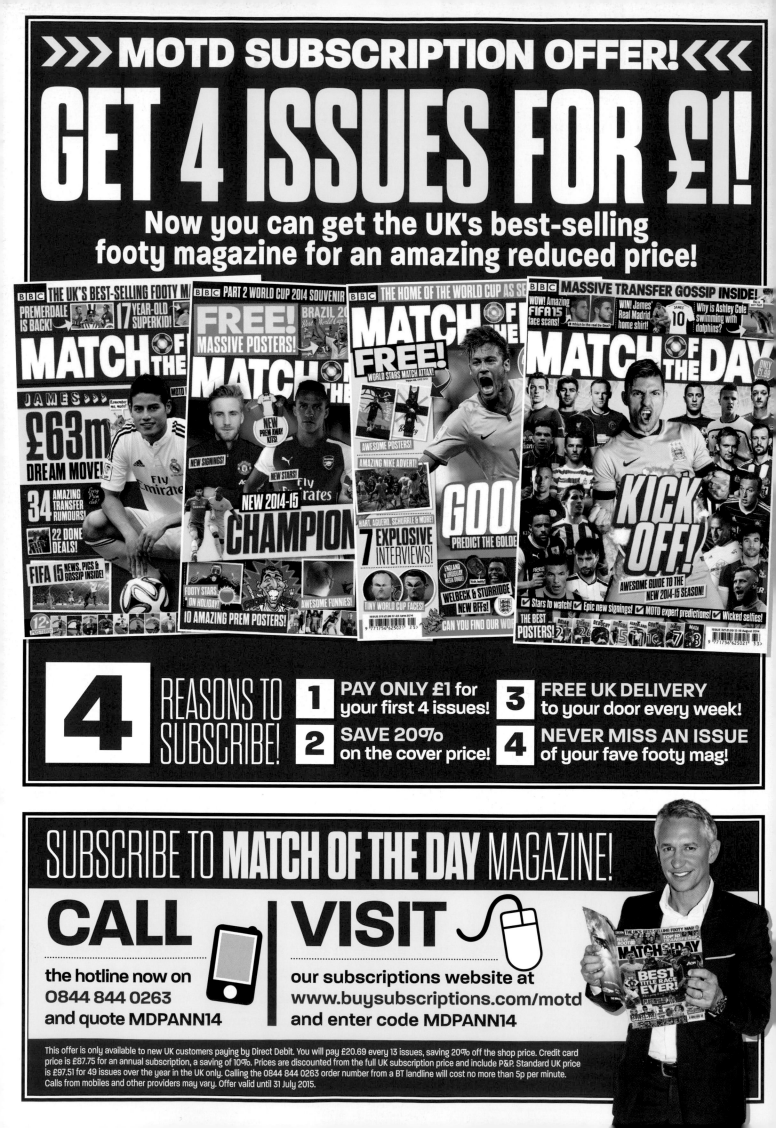

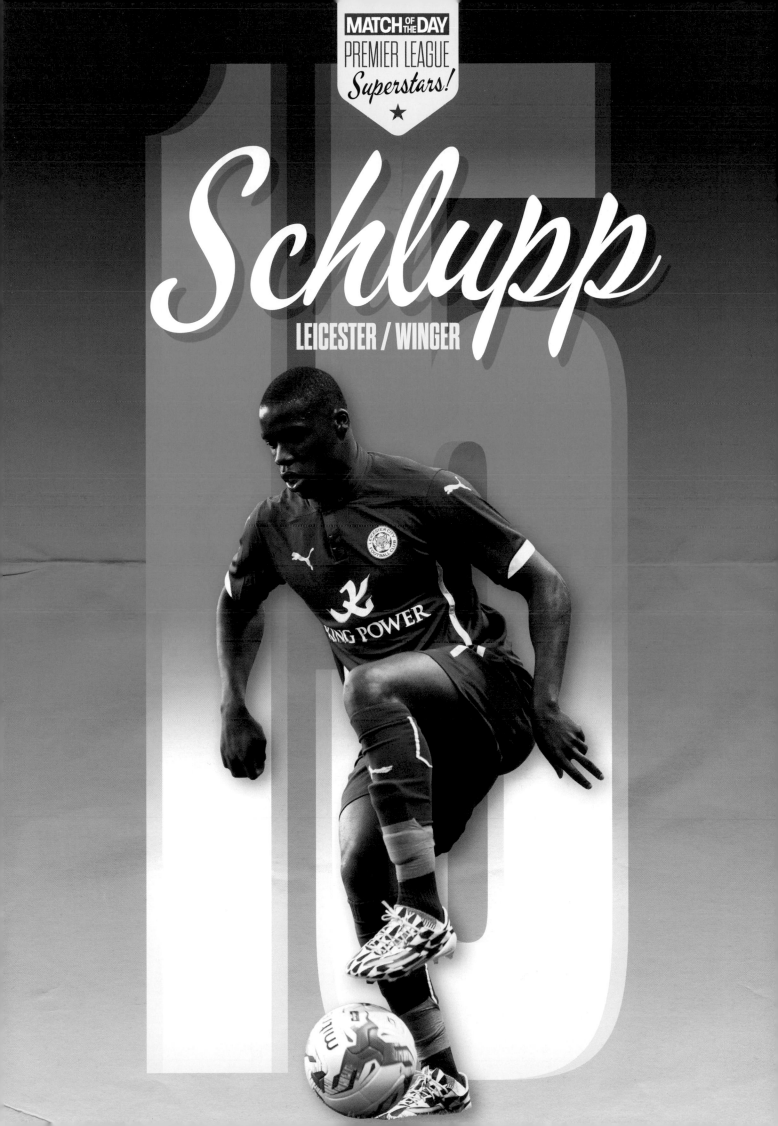

TOP 10

HOMES OF FOOTBALL!

MOTD reveals the Premier League's biggest stadiums!

Capacity 36,240

10 WHITE HART LANE TOTTENHAM

Tottenham's ground was built on the site of an old garden nursery in 1898. Originally it held just 5,000 fans but has expanded through the years to hold Olympic Games matches, England internationals and FA Cup semi-finals!

Capacity 39,572

9 GOODISON PARK EVERTON

Built 122 years ago, Goodison is one of the oldest grounds in the world. It has hosted more top-flight games than any other ground in England. One of the host stadiums for the 1966 World Cup, it also held the FA Cup final way back in 1910!

Capacity 41,841

8 STAMFORD BRIDGE CHELSEA

Before its renovation in the 1990s, a dog track ran around the outside of the pitch and one stand was essentially a shed. These days, it's a glitzy, modern, all-seater stadium with hotels and restaurants built into its structure!

Capacity 42,682

7 VILLA PARK ASTON VILLA

Villa Park is another grand, old stadium of English football, built 117 years ago in 1897. It's hosted cycling, athletics and more FA Cup semi-finals than any other stadium, as well as the last-ever UEFA Cup Winners' Cup final in 1999!

Capacity 45,522

6 ANFIELD LIVERPOOL

Anfield was originally the home of Everton until they were chucked out over a rent dispute in 1891, and a year later Liverpool moved in. Famous for its Kop stand, Anfield creates one of the best atmospheres in English footy!

Capacity 47,405

5 ETIHAD STADIUM MAN. CITY

This wicked stadium was originally built for use in the 2002 Commonwealth Games. Now, City are the permanent residents and have won two Prem titles since they moved in. They plan to expand the capacity to 55,000 in 2015!

Capacity 48,707

4 STADIUM OF LIGHT SUNDERLAND

The Mackems moved here from Roker Park in 1997 and it has hosted concerts by Rihanna and Coldplay. The stadium shares its name with Benfica's ground in Portugal, and was chosen as a tribute to the region's mine workers!

Capacity 52,404

3 ST JAMES' PARK NEWCASTLE

Smack bang in the middle of Newcastle, this enormous white structure rises out of the city like some sort of space station. In its 122-year history The Toon have won four league titles, the last of which came long ago in 1927!

Capacity 60,362

2 EMIRATES STADIUM ARSENAL

This superbowl is a far cry from the cramped, old Highbury, where Arsenal played until 2006. Built for £390 million, the Emirates was the personal dream of Arsene Wenger, who even helped design the dressing rooms!

1

Capacity 75,731

OLD TRAFFORD MAN. UNITED

Ah, the Theatre of Dreams! Bobby Charlton, George Best, David Beckham, Cristiano Ronaldo – they've all strutted their stuff at this 105-year-old stadium. Second World War bombing actually forced the temporary closure of Old Trafford in 1941 – but nothing could keep this old beauty down for ever!

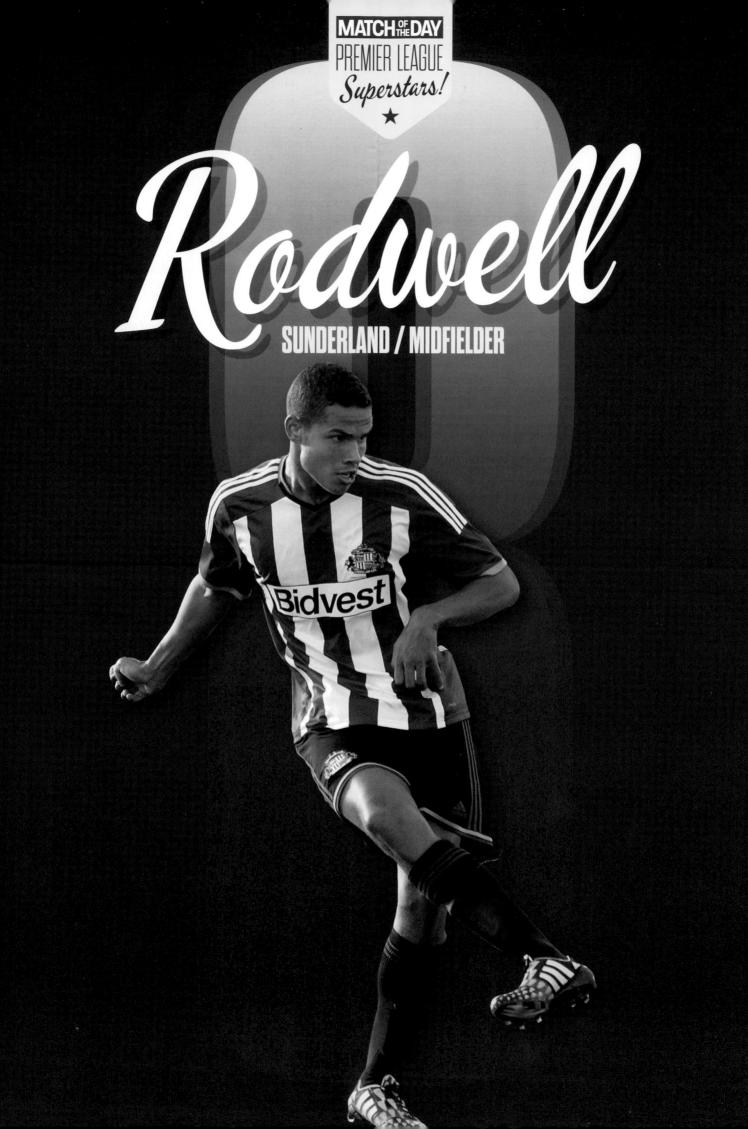

Rodwell

SUNDERLAND / MIDFIELDER

7 WONDERS OF THE WORLD

GLOBAL MEGASTARS ALERT!

Since Ancient times, man has created a list of the seven most spectacular creations on the planet. Now it's our turn!

WHAT MAKES A WONDER?

GREAT BEAUTY
It's got to be a pleasure to watch!

HISTORICAL IMPACT
It must have left its mark on the world!

WORLD RECOGNITION
It's got to be well-known the world over!

MUST-SEE STATUS
Seeing it is guaranteed to be memorable!

▶▶▶ **TURN OVER TO SEE WHO'S MADE OUR LIST!**

WONDER No.1
ARJEN ROBBEN

DISCOVERED IN: GRONINGEN, NORTH-EAST HOLLAND

NOW FOUND IN: MUNICH, SOUTH GERMANY

STATISTICS

MADE IN: BEDUM, HOLLAND, 1984

HEIGHT: 5FT 11IN

AGE: 30

ESTIMATED WORTH: £50 MILLION

Wonder features: Sprint-dribbling, powerful left-foot

■ Most people slow down as they get older, but not this guy. Robben was clocked dribbling at 23mph at the World Cup, making him the fastest footballer on the planet. Whatever you do, don't let him onto that left foot!

WONDER No.2
LIONEL MESSI

DISCOVERED IN: ROSARIO, CENTRAL ARGENTINA

NOW FOUND IN: BARCELONA, NORTH-EAST SPAIN

STATISTICS

MADE IN: ROSARIO, ARGENTINA, 1987 HEIGHT: 5FT 7IN

AGE: 27

ESTIMATED WORTH: £200 MILLION

Wonder features: Pinpoint passing, magical left-foot, dribbling

■ Messi is like one of those cartoon mice who squeezes through a hole in the wall that never quite looked big enough. For Messi, those holes are in the defences of the best teams in the world. What a star!

MORE WONDERS!

This lot have all been included on a Seven Wonders Of The World list at some point!

STONEHENGE
Pre-historic monument
Wiltshire, UK

COLOSSEUM
Roman amphitheatre
Rome, Italy

SUPER C-RON!

WONDER No.3
CRISTIANO RONALDO

DISCOVERED IN: FUNCHAL, ISLAND OF MADEIRA

NOW FOUND IN: MADRID, CENTRAL SPAIN

STATISTICS

MADE IN: FUNCHAL, MADEIRA, PORTUGAL, 1985 **HEIGHT:** 6FT 1IN

AGE: 29

ESTIMATED WORTH: £150 MILLION

Wonder features: Unique tricks, stampeding dribbles, power shooting

■ Ronaldo has invented so many new techniques, he's practically created a new sport. Before him, nobody struck those dipping free-kicks like he did or attempted step-overs at full-speed. There's no-one quite like him!

WONDER No.4
ALEXIS SANCHEZ

DISCOVERED IN: CALAMA, NORTH CHILE

NOW FOUND IN: LONDON, SOUTH-EAST ENGLAND

STATISTICS

MADE IN: TOCOPILLA, CHILE, 1988 **HEIGHT:** 5FT 7IN

AGE: 25

ESTIMATED WORTH: £35 MILLION

Wonder features: Clever finishing, piercing dribbles, darting runs

■ He comes from the desert in the north of Chile, but there's nothing dry about watching this trickster. At the World Cup in 2014 he showed his close control and lung-bursting runs could take him to the highest level!

GREAT PYRAMID OF GIZA
Ancient tomb
Giza, Egypt

TAJ MAHAL
Indian temple
Agra, India

GREAT WALL OF CHINA
Huge wall
Throughout China

▶▶▶ TURN OVER TO SEE MORE WONDERS!

WONDER No.5
GARETH BALE

DISCOVERED IN: CARDIFF, SOUTH WALES

NOW FOUND IN: MADRID, CENTRAL SPAIN

STATISTICS

MADE IN: CARDIFF, WALES, 1989

AGE: 25

HEIGHT: 6FT

ESTIMATED WORTH: £85 MILLION

Wonder features: Classy left foot, kick-and-run acceleration

■ There's an old-fashioned thrill in watching Bale do his work on a football pitch. Sure, he's got some flicks and tricks, but his most exciting move is to knock it past defenders and roast them in a classic foot race!

WONDER No.6
NEYMAR

NIFTY NEYMAR!

DISCOVERED IN: SAO PAULO, SOUTH-EAST BRAZIL

NOW FOUND IN: BARCELONA, NORTH-EAST SPAIN

STATISTICS

MADE IN: MOGI DAS CRUZES, BRAZIL, 1992

AGE: 22

HEIGHT: 5FT 9IN

ESTIMATED WORTH: £100 MILLION

Wonder features: Ground-breaking skill, high-speed dribbling

■ You never know what's coming next with Neymar. It could be a mischievous nutmeg that never looked possible, a spot of wildly outrageous in-game juggling or an unstoppable power-drive – he's a genius!

EVEN MORE WONDERS!

This lot have all been included on a Seven Wonders Of The World list at some point!

ZEUS
Greek statue
Olympia, Greece

LEANING TOWER OF PISA
Cathedral bell tower
Pisa, Italy

JAMES FACTS!
→ Had a mild stutter as a child!
→ Made his pro debut aged 15!
→ Helped Banfield win their first-ever Argentinian title!
→ His £38.5m move to Monaco made him the most expensive player in French footy history!

WONDER No.7
JAMES RODRIGUEZ

DISCOVERED IN: CUCUTA, NORTH-EAST COLOMBIA

NOW FOUND IN: MADRID, CENTRAL SPAIN

STATISTICS

MADE IN: CUCUTA, COLOMBIA, 1991 HEIGHT: 5FT 11IN

AGE: 23

ESTIMATED WORTH: £70 MILLION

Wonder features: Exquisite left foot, gliding runs, silky finishing

■ The sights of James bewitching clueless defenders, or blitzing a perfect volley into the top corner are two of the greatest in world football today! He has showcased his skills in club football in Colombia, Argentina, Portugal and France, but it was his classy six-goal wonder-show in Brazil in 2014 that wowed the watching world!

HANGING GARDENS OF BABYLON
Ancient garden
Location, unknown

EMPIRE STATE BUILDING
Skyscraper
New York, USA

CHRIST THE REDEEMER
Statue
Rio De Janeiro, Brazil

FOOTBALL LEAGUE
Crossword!

It's not all about the Premier League y'know! How clued up are you on the Football League?

8 DOWN

6 DOWN

GET THE ANSWERS ON p92!

ACROSS

2 Mick McCarthy is the manager of this club! (7)
5 The city that Leyton Orient are from! (6)
7 Adam Le Fondre plays for this club! (7)
8 The team that won League 2 last season! (12)
10 Alex Pritchard is on loan at Brentford from this Prem club! (9)
11 The colour of the Nottingham Forest home shirt! (3)

DOWN

1 This current Championship team won the FA Cup in 2013! (5)
3 Sheffield Wednesday captain Glenn Loovens is from this country! (7)
4 Norwich's nickname is The _____! (8)
6 Ross _____ joined Fulham for £11 million in the summer! (9)
8 The Sheffield United manager is Nigel _____! (6)
9 Leeds play their home games at _____ Road! (6)

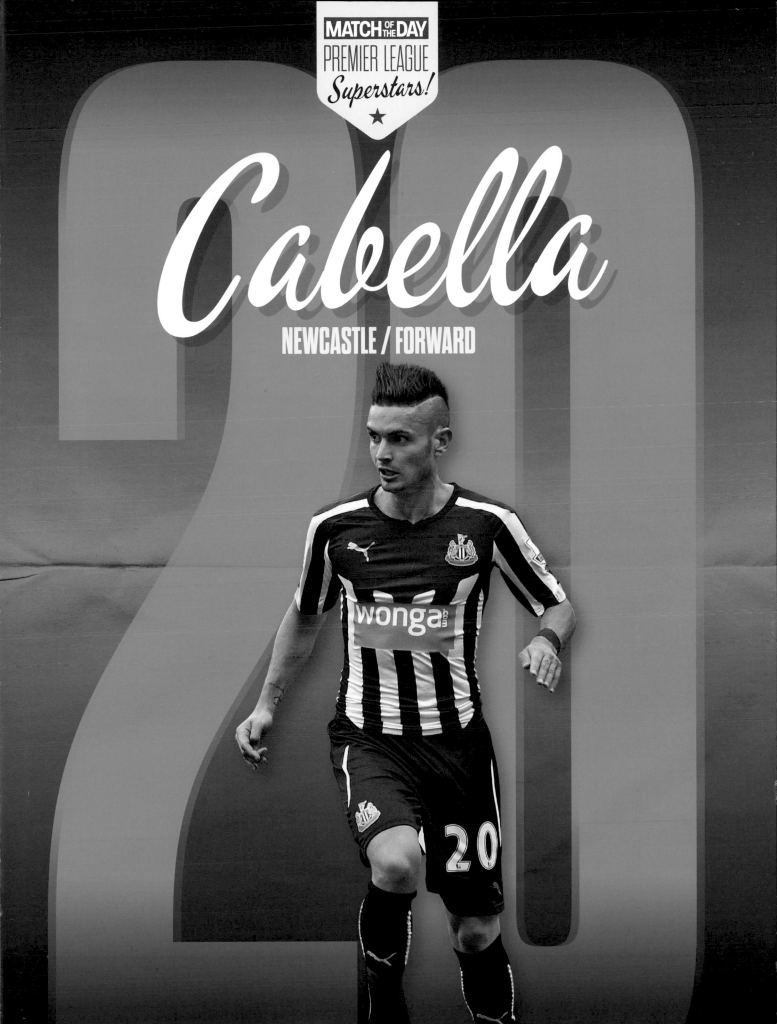

Cabella

NEWCASTLE / FORWARD

★ THE BIG DEBATE ★ THE BIG DEBATE ★ THE BIG DEBATE ★

WILL ENGLAND EVER WIN THE WORLD CUP?

It's now been 48 years since England won the World Cup so we got Paz & Bez to debate whether they'll EVER do it again!

 PAZ SAYS: **NO!**   BEZ SAYS: **YES!**

"TRUST ME, WE WON'T!"

Paz says:
"Trust me, I've been watching England for a long time and while we've always had talented players, we just can't turn them into a team that's capable of holding it together on the big stage. I just can't see that changing. Nobody knows why – it's just one of those great mysteries of the universe!"

"TIMES ARE CHANGING!"

Bez says:
"But times are changing, Paz! You saw the way Raheem Sterling stuck it to the Italians, and Ross Barkley played with no fear against Uruguay, too. This new generation aren't scared of their responsibilities. They'll step up!"

"ROY'S NO GOOD!"

Paz says: "Not with Roy Hodgson in charge, they won't! He made so many mistakes at the World Cup. I haven't even got time to list them all now – he should have had an extra man in central midfield for starters. If he stays in charge it'll be the same old story – we'll get nowhere!"

● Gerrard will be a big loss for The Three Lions!

"PROBLEM SOLVED!"

Bez says: "Hang on a minute! Weren't we all saying he should start with an attacking line-up? He picked an exciting team, which is more than previous managers have done. Sure they were open in midfield, but that was mostly down to Stevie G's creaking knees. Now he's gone, it's problem solved!"

"WHO REPLACES STEVIE G?"

Paz says:
"Come on then, who replaces Stevie G? I agree with you that he was past his best, but we haven't exactly got a queue of world-class replacements in that central midfield position, have we? The best teams, Spain, Argentina and the Germans, take control of the midfield. We just cannot seem to do that!"

"I SEE GLORY!'"

Bez says:
"That's where you're wrong, Paz! When I look to the future I see a wicked midfield three of Jordan Henderson, Ross Barkley and Jack Wilshere. They've got skill, energy and that bit of bite you need at the top level. They'll drive us on to World Cup glory, I'm sure of it. Well, sort of!"

ROONEY!

THE BEST
OF THE REST!

A look back at England's best World Cup efforts!

1966

WINNERS
Bobby Moore led The Three Lions to an epic 4-2 win over Germany in the final on home soil!

1990

SEMI-FINALS
England came so close to reaching another final, but were dumped out by the Germans on pens!

2002

QUARTER-FINALS
Michael Owen gave England the lead against Brazil, but the Brazilians snatched a 2-1 win!

WHO DO YOU AGREE WITH?
Are you TEAM PAZ or TEAM BEZ? Join the debate by emailing us at pazandbez@motdmag.com and we'll print the best arguments in the mag!

Agbonlahor

ASTON VILLA / FORWARD

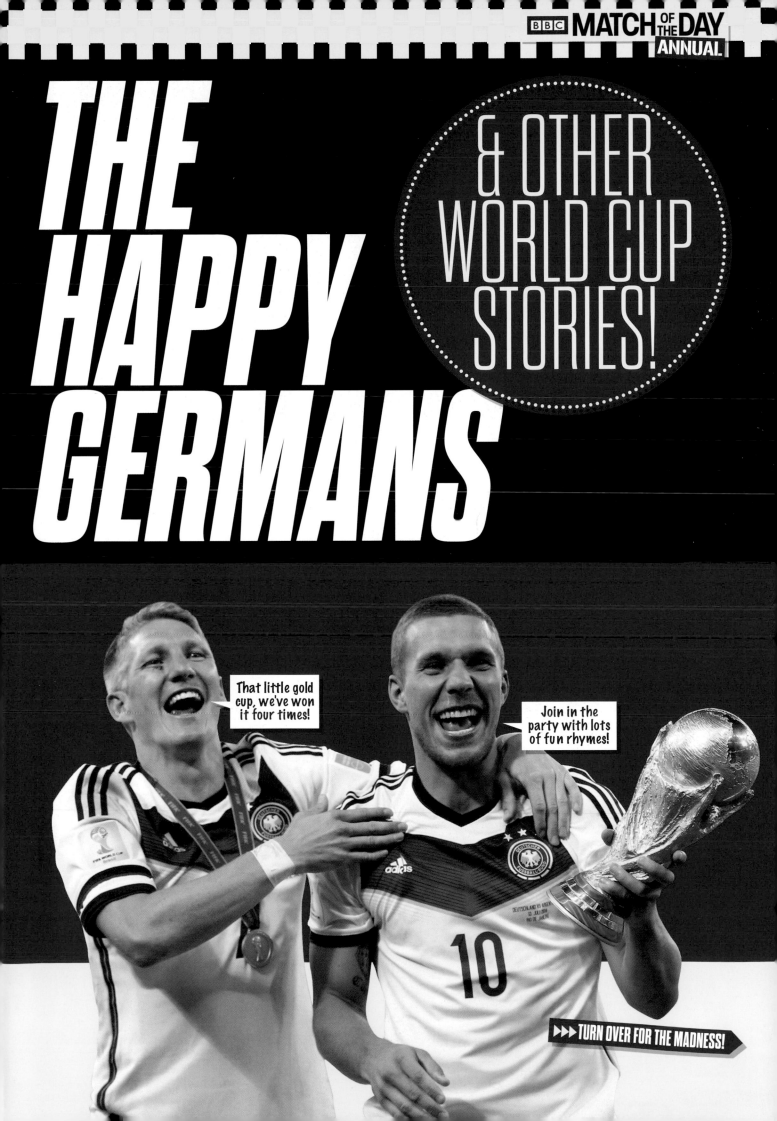

The Super Duper Suitcase

*The super duper suitcase
was filled with cash
and gold,
Flown all the way from
Ghana, for the players
we were told!*

*Would they start to play
much better, now the
riches had arrived?
No, they scored own goals
and lost, with their poor
supporters left deprived!*

THE BOY WHO GOT CROCKED

*The boy who got crocked
had an up and down time,
Early on, scoring goals was
his only real crime!*

*He swished that left
boot and brought a
country pure joy,
Neymar, the trickster, the
showman, the boy!*

But as the final loomed

*close, there was
tension and fear,
When a reckless
old hoof ended up
costing him dear!*

*The Colombian tackle left
a nation so shocked,
And Neymar was soon
just the boy who
got crocked!*

THE HAPPY GERMA

En una noche en Rio

On an evening in Rio,
the south of Brazil,
Some Germans did well, and
beat Argentina one-nil!

They'd waited for years
for this little gold cup,
For their captain Phil Lahm
to lift it right up!

For ages it was close and
no-one could score,
But still those good Germans
did knock on the door!
Then boss Jogi Low, he did
make a swift change,
Gotze came on and he
scored from close range!

The party was started right
there on the pitch,
Those 11 Happy Germans
scratched their World Cup itch!

BOY OH BOY, ROY

Boy oh boy, Roy,
What on earth was your ploy?

Sure, we all got a buzz from
the rise of Raheem,
But it seemed you'd forgotten
the rest of the team?

Gerrard looked old and
he lacked any vision,
His pairing with Hendo
needed nuclear fission!

Then Wayne once again
left us really insane,
Boy, oh boy, Roy,
please end all this pain!

What A Pain For Spain

What a pain for Spain
That they ended their reign,
With nothing so much
as a quiet refrain!

No tiki
No taka,
No passing
No fun,
It was like some strange
nightmare,
Wake us up when
they're done!

▶▶▶ **TURN OVER FOR MORE MADNESS!**

LEAN & GREEN, THE AFRICAN MACHINE

That Algerian kit –
was it green or spearmint?
Whatever it was, they
gave us no hint!
That they'd push those big
Germans right up to the end,
By then they could count
MOTD as a friend!
They were strong, they were
quick, they were lean,
and, yes, green!
From now on we'll call them
The African Machine!

We'll Score And We'll Score And Then We'll Score More

Don't play the Germans
when you're falling apart,
There's no charity –
they go straight for the heart!

First Muller, then Klose,
then Kroos, then two more,
One thing's for sure, it wasn't a bore!

As they rattled in seven
without much reply,
The Brazilians traipsed
home for a jolly good cry!

JUMPING FOR JOY WITH JAMES

We just couldn't help but
start jumping for James,
And not just because he's
got one of our names!

That volley he crashed
in just under the bar,
Confirmed to the world
that this guy was a star!

Controlled on his chest,
not even facing the goal,
He swivelled and hit, with
all heart and much soul!

When the ball hit the net
we were all on our feet,
Jumping for Joy with James
gets you out of your seat!

The ones that go wheeee!

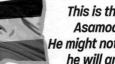

This is the story of
Asamoah Gyan,
He might not score goals,
he will and he can!

And not just the tap-ins
you've come to expect,
Of those journeymen
strikers when put to the test!

He gets belters, ripsnorters,
the ones that go wheeee!

Like that memorable
sidefoot, against
Germany!

A DOLLOP OF WALLOP

From the land of old
Oz, where they stand
upside down!

Came a man on
a mission, this guy
was no clown!

He scored against Chile,
a header no less,
But it wasn't till Holland
when we saw his best!

That volley, that strike,
his greatest thus far,
A dollop of wallop you
don't find in a jar!

>>> TURN OVER FOR MORE MADNESS!

IS THAT AN OCTOPUS?

Is that an Octopus,
Crouching down there?
The one in the black shirt,
With the big mop of hair.

No, of course not, you fool,
It's that flexible goalie,
You know, that one who the
Mexicans stand up and olē!

Remember Brazil?
He made save after save!
Do you think a real octopus
Would be really so brave?

If Bryan Can Do It...

If Bryan can do it, then you can and I can,
Not least when you look at
the stats from his lifespan!

Eight goals for The Cottagers,
Five more out on loan!

Then he scored against Italy,
And sent England home!

HE'LL DRIBBL AND DRIBBL

Well, that Arjen Robben,
he'll dribble and dribble.

With that you'll find no
man to argue or quibble!

He'll dribble
past Xavi,
past Ramos,
past Iker!

He's a slippery one –
a right little sneaker!

He did it to Spain and
he'll do it to you.

But when he gets on a roll,
there's nothing to do!

AND DRIBBLE AND DRIBBLE

The Frogman Of Mexico

The frogman of Mexico,
He jerks and he croaks!

He high-fives his players,
Like he's one of the blokes!

Raising hell on the touchline,
He bawls and he yells!

We're amazed their FA
got him in for two spells!

YELLOW FELLOWS WHO DANCE

Have you seen the
yellow fellows?
How they prance
and they dance!

They jiggle
and wriggle,
When they get the chance!

It's the man called Armero,
Who leads these young men,
But you'll wait four
more years,
Till you see it again!

▶▶▶ TURN OVER FOR MORE MADNESS!

THERE WAS A BALD MAN FROM NEW JERSEY

There was a bald man from New Jersey,
Who could probably keep out Van Persie!

Against Belgium he saved,
While the world watched and raved,

And the bald man refused to show mercy!

You Can't Stop Mr Klose

You can't stop Mr Klose,
However hard you try!

Be wary of his danger,
Or he'll hang you out to dry!

He's now a record-breaker,
With 15 World Cup goals!

And to think, if not for a twist of fate,
He'd have scored them for the Poles!

HE HAD A ROCKET IN HIS POCKET

He had a rocket in his
pocket, that David Luiz,
It would explode unannounced
like a ruddy big sneeze!

Against Colombia
in the quarters,
He walked up to sock it,
And out came that rocket
he kept in his pocket!

My Whopper Grasshopper

My whopper grasshopper
will sit on my knee,
But not if I'm taking a big penalty!

For then he'll hop up and
settle down on my shoulder,
It's unknown to me when he
became so much bolder!

But lucky for me he
seems quite the charm,
I've never missed from the
spot with that boy on my arm!

I COULD EAT AN ITALIAN TODAY

"I could eat an Italian today,"
thought the
troublesome striker,
Before heading out to play!

Sadly for Luis,
he took only one bite,
Before his Italian delicacy
jumped up to fight!

It wasn't the last shock
poor Suarez did feel,
As FIFA banned him for ages
to bring him to heel!

Who is the BEST OF ALL TIME?

MARADONA

ONE-MAN MATCH-WINNING MACHINE!

Full name: Diego Armando Maradona Franco
Date of birth: 30 October, 1960
Place of birth: Buenos Aires, Argentina
Height: 5ft 5in **Strongest foot:** Left

CLUB CAREER

Years	Team	Games	Goals
1976-1981	Argentinos Juniors	166	116
1981-1982	Boca Juniors	40	28
1982-1984	Barcelona	58	38
1984-1991	Napoli	259	115
1992-1993	Sevilla	29	8
1993-1994	Newell's Old Boys	5	0
1995-1997	Boca Juniors	31	7

INTERNATIONAL CAREER

Years	Team	Games	Goals
1977-1994	Argentina	91	34

PLAYING STYLE

A classic No.10, known for his dribbling, vision, ball control and creativity!

TROPHY CABINET

Won 1986 World Cup and league titles in Italy and Argentina!

SUPPORTERS SAY:

"His displays in the 1986 World Cup were the greatest ever in a footy tournament!"

CRITICS SAY:

"He was a cheat – should that ever be forgotten?"

PELE

FOOTBALL'S FIRST GLOBAL SUPERSTAR!

Full name: Edson Arantes Do Nascimento
Date of birth: 21 October, 1940
Place of birth: Tres Coracoes, Brazil
Height: 5ft 8in **Strongest foot:** Right

CLUB CAREER

Years	Team	Games	Goals
1956-1974	Santos	656	643
1975-1977	New York Cosmos	107	64

INTERNATIONAL CAREER

Years	Team	Games	Goals
1957-1971	Brazil	92	77

PLAYING STYLE

A powerful, skilful all-round forward who could play as a striker or at No.10 – scored loads of goals and bagged tons of assists!

TROPHY CABINET

He won the World Cup a record three times. At club level, he won two South American championships and six Brazilian titles!

SUPPORTERS SAY:

"He was the complete player, awesome in the air, incredible on the ground and his scoring record is second to none!"

CRITICS SAY:

"The Brazil teams he played in were so good his job was easy – plus he only ever played club football in Brazil and the USA!"

MESSI

A GOAL-SCORING, DRIBBLING PHENOMENON!

Full name: Lionel Andres Messi Cuccittini
Date of birth: 24 June, 1987
Place of birth: Rosario, Argentina
Height: 5ft 7in **Strongest foot:** Left

CLUB CAREER

Years	Team	Games	Goals
2004-	Barcelona	425	354

INTERNATIONAL CAREER

Years	Team	Games	Goals
2005-	Argentina	93	42

PLAYING STYLE

An explosive dribbler who can burst past five defenders in an instant before thumping a shot into the net!

TROPHY CABINET

Three Champions Leagues and six La Liga winners' medals!

SUPPORTERS SAY:

"He's destroying every record there is – the main man for the greatest club team in history!"

CRITICS SAY:

"Pele and Maradona won the World Cup – Messi still hasn't done that!"

MOTD VERDICT!
1st Messi
2nd Maradona
3rd Pele

MY VERDICT!
1st
2nd
3rd

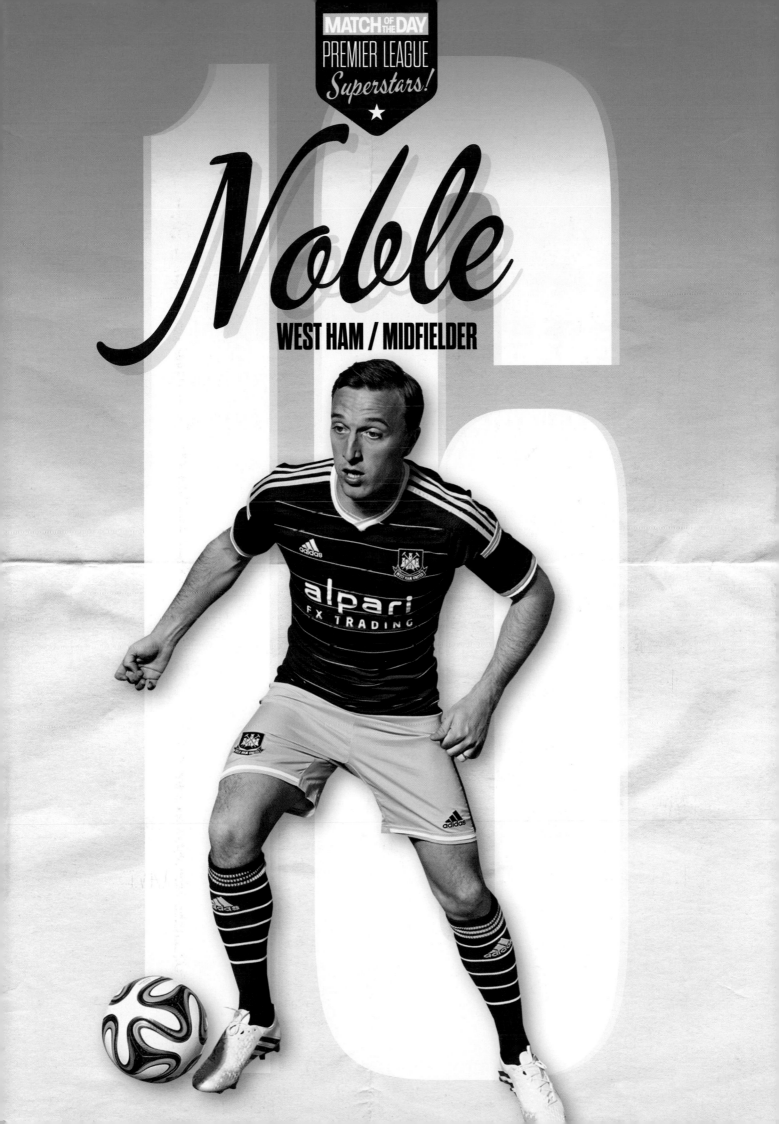

AROUND THE WORLD IN 50 QUESTIONS!

GET THE ANSWERS ON p92!

Strap yourselves in and get ready for a tour of questions on footy-mad countries. In case of emergency, exits can be found on both sides of the magazine. Thank you for choosing Match Of The Day Airways!

▶▶▶ TURN OVER TO START!

SPAIN

Meet the Spaniards!

Match the player to the fact about them!

1 He has played two friendlies for Brazil!
ANSWER

2 Chelsea signed him in 2012 for £7 million!
ANSWER

3 Spain's most-capped player of all time!
ANSWER

4 He has won six league titles with Barcelona!
ANSWER

5 He's won the Champions League with Liverpool!
ANSWER

LA LIGA Superstars!

Name these top players from the Spanish league, por favor!

1 BALE

2 MESSI

3 ANSWER

4 XAVI

5 RONALDO

6 ANSWER

7 ANSWER

8 PEPE

GERMANY

GET THE ANSWERS ON p92!

★★★ Meet the Germans!
Match the player to the fact about them!

1
He was at Man. City for one season!
ANSWER

2
He was the top scorer at the 2010 World Cup!
ANSWER

3
Moved to the Prem in 2013 in a £42.5 million deal!
ANSWER

4
He is the top scorer in World Cup history!
ANSWER

5
He is the captain of Bayern Munich!
ANSWER

BUNDESLIGA Superstars!
Name these top players from ze German league!

1 ANSWER

2 ANSWER

3 ANSWER

4 ROBBEN

5 ANSWER

6 ANSWER

7 ANSWER

8 ANSWER

ITALY

Meet the Italians!

Match the player to the fact about them!

1 This guy was bitten by Luis Suarez at the World Cup!

ANSWER

2 He joined Borussia Dortmund in June this year!

ANSWER

3 Oldest outfield player in Italy's World Cup squad!

ANSWER

4 He's the most-capped player in Italy's history!

ANSWER

5 He won the Premier League with Man. City in 2012!

ANSWER

SERIE A Superstars!

Name these top players from the Italian league, per favore!

1 ANSWER

2 ANSWER

3 ANSWER

4 ANSWER

5 ANSWER

6 ANSWER

7 ANSWER

8 ANSWER

WHERE ARE THEY?

Match the football clubs to the city they come from!

A

B

F

G

C

E

D

| 1 Galatasaray | 2 Porto | 3 PSG | 4 Ajax | 5 Basel | 6 Barcelona | 7 Celtic |

NAME THE COUNTRY!

Which national football teams do these badges belong to?

GET THE ANSWERS ON p92!

1 ANSWER

2 ANSWER

3 ANSWER

4 ANSWER

50 YEARS OF MATCH OF THE DAY!

DID YOU KNOW?
The first-ever words were: "Welcome to Match Of The Day, the first of a weekly series coming to you every Saturday on BBC Two!"

DID YOU KNOW?
At the start, MOTD was a one-off series, a trial run for the 1966 World Cup!

MOTD TIMELINE!

1964
The first-ever Match Of The Day is broadcast on BBC Two – but only 20,000 people tune in to watch!

1966
The show gets a big Saturday night slot on BBC One after England's World Cup triumph!

1968
The show starts to pull in five million viewers per week – it's getting more and more popular!

1969
Wowsers – the show is broadcast in colour for the first time in its short history!

Back in August 1964, the first-ever Match Of The Day episode was broadcast. To celebrate the show's epic 50th birthday, we're taking you back in time!

Kenneth Wolstenholme, the commentator who went on to say "They think it's all over, it is now" at the 1966 World Cup final, was the first host of MOTD!

Jimmy Hill and Bob Wilson hard at work in the days when the studio was made from Lego!

Hill also presented MOTD from a cave back in the 1970s!

In the 1990s, host Des Lynam regularly refused to join in with the lads' No Blazer Day!

Alan Hansen and Gary Lineker – don't mess!

Lineker and Hansen after being told there are no crisps left!

1970 The famous, and now much-loved, MOTD theme tune is launched!

1971 The new video-disc allows slo-mo replays – while commentator John Motson makes his MOTD debut!

1973 Jimmy Hill signs from ITV to front the programme alongside ex-Arsenal keeper Bob Wilson!

1980 The show moves to a Sunday afternoon slot, before returning to Saturdays a year later!

1982 Another switch to Sunday afternoons for everyone's fave footy show Match Of The Day!

50 YEARS OF MATCH OF THE DAY!

What does MOTD mean to you, Gary?

Lineker says: "I grew up with Match Of The Day like everyone else. It's great that it's still hugely popular after all these years. It's great that people still find it a great watch. And it shows that highlights still work in this modern era of so much live football!"

What about your own childhood memories of MOTD?

Lineker says: "When I was growing up it was the only way you could see football on TV. You might get the FA Cup final and the odd European match but not much else. So it was an integral part of TV viewing when I was younger, for me and a lot of people!"

Do you remember your first TV appearance?

Lineker says: "I remember my first night vividly. It was a Euro 1996 highlights show – I was terrified! There's no way you can practise anything like that. A live show, people talking in your ear while you're dealing with cameras and knowing where to look!"

But it couldn't have gone too badly!

Lineker says: "I wasn't very good but I wasn't bad enough that they kicked me off! You become familiar with live TV, you become yourself, then you're relaxed and people will decide if they like you or not!"

EXCLUSIVE INTERVIEW WITH AN MOTD LEGEND!

GARY LINEKER
MOTD PRESENTER 1999-PRESENT

1983
MOTD is joined on the BBC by live league football – but a strike by technical staff blanks out four shows!

1988
The BBC signs a deal to show the FA Cup. The show is renamed Match Of The Day: The Road to Wembley!

1992
League footy is back on Match Of The Day. Alan Hansen makes his MOTD debut!

2000
ITV win the rights to show Prem highlights from the beginning of the 2001-02 season!

2001
Match Of The Day continues with action from the FA Cup and England internationals!

WHAT ELSE HAPPENED IN 1964?

All this stuff happened the same year as the first MOTD!

- Harry Hill was born!
- BBC Two started broadcasting in Great Britain!
- The Rolling Stones released their debut album!
- The Beatles had their first US No.1!
- West Ham won the first of their three FA Cups!

WHAT HADN'T HAPPENED BY 1964?

- England had NOT won the World Cup – it happened two years later!
- Man had NOT set foot on the moon – it happened five years later!
- The Internet had NOT been invented – it happened 27 years later!

EXCLUSIVE INTERVIEW WITH AN MOTD LEGEND!

ALAN SHEARER
MOTD PUNDIT 2006-PRESENT

Alan, what are your childhood memories of MOTD?

Shearer says: "I watched it all the time with my parents. To be on it now is a huge honour. The 2006 World Cup was my first tournament. It was great!"

Were you nervous for your first time on TV?

Shearer says: "I did get nervous when I started because it's live TV, you're not allowed to make a mistake. You get used to it, though. It still gives me a buzz but it's very different to playing in front of 80,000 fans!"

WATCH IT!

MATCH OF THE DAY and **MATCH OF THE DAY 2** Saturdays and Sundays, on BBC One! Catch all the highlights from every weekend of Premier League action!

BBC One

2004
Premier League highlights return to the BBC, and MOTD2 starts on BBC Two, hosted by Adrian Chiles!

2007
Jacqui Oatley becomes the first woman to commentate on a Match Of The Day game!

2011
MOTD leaves its London home and moves to a hi-tech studio in Salford with the rest of BBC Sport!

2012
MOTD2 proves to be a big hit and moves from BBC Two to BBC One!

2014
MOTD celebrates 50 amazing years of delivering the best footy coverage!

ANSWERS!

MOTD CROSSWORD! (p14)
ACROSS
4 Man City 7 Seventh
8 West Ham 10 Jagielka
12 Eleven
DOWN
1 Potters 2 KC 3 Spain
5 Pochettino 6 Benfica
9 Saints 11 Liberty

50/FIFTY! (p30)
1 B (cheetahs can reach speeds of 60-75mph – that's faster than any human) 2 B (the Queen is 24 years older than Arsene Wenger) 3 A (Crouch is 6ft 7in. Three Crouches would be 19ft 9in. Double-decker buses are 14ft 4in tall!)
4 B (EastEnders started in 1985. St Mary's was built in 2001)
5 A (Kumbuka weighs 29st. Together, Aguero and Negredo weigh 23st 5lb) 6 B (a football pitch is 105m long, while the Eiffel Tower is 301m tall)
7 A (it took £798m to build Wembley, but just £44.5m to make Despicable Me 2)
8 A (when we last checked, Wayne Rooney had scored more goals than Mr Bean!)

MIDDLE-NAME CONFESSIONS! (p34)
1 A, 2 C, 3 A, 4 B, 5 C, 6 A, 7 A, 8 C, 9 A.

● Wigan celebrate their shock victory over Man. City in the 2013 FA Cup Final!

TOP TOTS! (p56)
1 John Terry 2 Tim Krul 3 Arsene Wenger 4 Rob Green 5 Mauricio Pochettino 6 Rickie Lambert

FOOTBALL LEAGUE CROSSWORD! (p66)
ACROSS
2 Ipswich 5 London
7 Cardiff 8 Chesterfield

10 Tottenham
11 Red
DOWN
1 Wigan 3 Holland
4 Canaries 6 McCormack
8 Clough 11 Elland

AROUND THE WORLD IN 50 QUESTIONS! (p84–87)
MEET THE SPANIARDS!
1 C 2 D 3 A 4 E 5 B
LA LIGA SUPERSTARS!
1 Gareth Bale 2 Lionel Messi
3 Diego Godin 4 Xavi
5 Cristiano Ronaldo 6 Sergio Ramos 7 Neymar 8 Pepe
MEET THE GERMANS! 1 B 2 D 3 E 4 A 5 C
BUNDESLIGA SUPERSTARS!
1 Robert Lewandowski
2 Manuel Neuer 3 Ilkay Gundogan 4 Arjen Robben
5 Kevin-Prince Boateng
6 Franck Ribery 7 Marco Reus
8 Thiago Alcantara
MEET THE ITALIANS! 1 A 2 E 3 D 4 C 5 B
SERIE A SUPERSTARS!
1 Ashley Cole 2 Paul Pogba
3 Nemanja Vidic 4 Gonzalo Higuain 5 Carlos Tevez
6 Mario Gomez 7 Marek Hamsik 8 Gervinho
WHERE ARE THEY? 1 D 2 C 3 F 4 B 5 G 6 E 7 A
NAME THE COUNTRY! 1 Ivory Coast 2 Argentina 3 Australia
4 South Korea

● As a kid, Rickie Lambert supported Liverpool – now he plays for them!

● Kumbuka the gorilla – one of London Zoo's biggest attractions!

MATCH OF THE DAY MAGAZINE

THE BIGGEST SUPERSTARS EVERY WEEK!

Sterling

Van Persie

Aguero

Barkley

Ramsey

2012 MATCH OF THE DAY MAGAZINE AWARDS

VOTED BY MOTD READERS

Van Persie STRIKER OF THE YEAR 2012

THE UK'S BEST-SELLING FOOTY MAG!

MATCH OF THE DAY

Write to us at
Match Of The Day magazine
Immediate Media, Vineyard
House, 44 Brook Green,
Hammersmith,
London, W6 7BT

Telephone 020 7150 5121
Email shout@motdmag.com
pazandbez@motdmag.com
www.motdmag.com

Annual editor	Mark Parry	Picture hub assistant	Jo Crawford
Match Of The Day editor	Ian Foster	Production editor	Neil Queen-Jones
Art editor	Blue Buxton	Sub-editor	Joe Shackley
Deputy art editor	Lee Midwinter	Publishing consultant	Jaynie Bye
Designer	Nathan Battison	Editorial director	Corinna Shaffer
Senior features editor	Ed Bearryman	Annual images	PA Photos
Senior writer /		Contributers	Al Parr, Alex Brodie, David Lloyd,
web content editor	Richard Clare		David Preston
Group picture editor	Natasha Thompson	Thanks to	Gary Lineker, Alan Shearer,
Picture editor	Jason Timson		Paul Cemmick

BBC Books, an imprint of Ebury Publishing, 20 Vauxhall Bridge Road, London SW1V 2SA. BBC Books is part of the Penguin Random House group of companies whose addresses can be found at global.penguinrandomhouse.com. Copyright © Match Of The Day magazine, 2014. First published by BBC Books in 2014. www.eburypublishing.co.uk. A CIP catalogue record for this book is available from the British Library. ISBN 9781849908214. Commissioning editor: Albert DePetrillo, project editor: Lizzy Gaisford, production: Phil Spencer. Printed and bound in Germany by Mohn Media GmbH. Penguin Random House is committed to a sustainable future for our business, our readers and our planet. This book is made from Forest Stewardship Council ® certified paper.

The licence to publish this magazine was acquired from BBC Worldwide by Immediate Media Company on 1 November 2011. We remain committed to making a magazine of the highest editorial quality, one that complies with BBC editorial and commercial guidelines and connects with BBC programmes.

Match Of The Day Magazine is is published by Immediate Media Company London Limited, under licence from BBC Worldwide Limited.
© Immediate Media Company London Limited, 2014.

5 HEADLINES WE WANT TO READ IN 2015!

WAZZA HITS THE NET

MAN. UNITED star Wayne Rooney last night completed his controversial £1 billion takeover of YouTube – and immediately announced he was changing the name to RooTube.

FARMYARD SITCOM

The 28-year-old England striker also revealed RooTube will have exclusive rights to his new farmyard-based sitcom called Moo With Roo.

In a press conference, Rooney said: "With a quack, quack, here, and a quack, quack there!"

LAST-GASP LINEKER

GARY LINEKER marked his sensational return to top-flight football with an injury-time hat-trick last night.

The 53-year-old Match Of The Day presenter, who has come out of retirement to help former club Tottenham overcome their injury crisis, was also man of the match in the 3-2 win over north London rivals Arsenal.

CHUBBY

Tottenham supporter Roy Winston said: "Blimey, geez – he's still got it, hasn't he?"